READ BEFORE LEADING

20 Essential Leadership Lessons to Help you Succeed and Avoid Failure

Marc Hill

SMOKY COAST PRESS

Copyright © 2024 by Marc Hill & Smoky Coast Press

All rights reserved.

No portion of this book may be reproduced in any form without written permission from the publisher or author, except as permitted by U.S. copyright law.

This publication is designed to provide accurate and authoritative information in regard to the subject matter covered. It is sold with the understanding that neither the author nor the publisher is engaged in rendering legal, investment, accounting or other professional services. While the publisher and author have used their best efforts in preparing this book, they make no representations or warranties with respect to the accuracy or completeness of the contents of this book and specifically disclaim any implied warranties of merchantability or fitness for a particular purpose. No warranty may be created or extended by sales representatives or written sales materials. The advice and strategies contained herein may not be suitable for your situation. You should consult with a professional when appropriate. Neither the publisher nor the author shall be liable for any loss of profit or any other commercial damages, including but not limited to special, incidental, consequential, personal, or other damages.

Book Cover & illustrations by the author: Marc Hill

ISBN 979-8-9869893-8-9 (Paperback)

ISBN 979-8-9869893-7-2 (Hardcover)

ISBN 979-8-9869893-5-8 (eBook)

1st Edition, 2024

Acknowledgements

I want to first and foremost thank my beautiful and awesome wife, Sara. She has supported me through all of my writing and has been my number-one editor and honest reviewer. I couldn't have done this without her.

I also want to thank my ARC team for their thoughts and ideas, they made a big difference in the flow and organization of the book.

Dedication

This book is dedicated to all those out there who are looking to make a difference and help their organizations move forward.

Keep pushing and stay positive!

ALSO BY

Two Dark Thirty: True Stories to Inspire Teaching and Learning in Our Local Heroes

An all-encompassing guide for firefighter training, education, fire officer development, and instructing EMTs and paramedics. Written by an experienced firefighter and educator, this book blends real-world experiences with academic theories and educational principles, making it a crucial resource for first responder training and leadership development.

Two Dark Thirty: Companion Workbook

An interactive guide designed to complement "Two Dark Thirty: True Stories to Inspire Teaching and Learning in Our Local Heroes," this workbook offers practical exercises and reflections to help readers deepen their understanding, enhance their teaching abilities, and promote personal and professional growth.

Two Dark Thirty's All In One Firefighter Exam Preparation Book

Ensure your success by preparing with "Two Dark Thirty's All in One Firefighter Exam Preparation Book." This comprehensive guide is designed to help you achieve top scores on your firefighter exam, covering all essential topics and providing over 500 practice questions.

Read Before Leading: Companion Workbook

A hands-on guide inspired by the lessons of Read Before Leading, this workbook dives into 20 essential lessons to help leaders avoid common pitfalls and drive real success. Through reflective exercises, scenario-based challenges, and practical strategies, each lesson is designed to build core skills in humility, integrity, and resilience. Drawing on real-life experiences, this workbook guides leaders to navigate complex team dynamics, find work-life balance, and make ethical decisions, all while inspiring their teams and staying true to their values.

CONTENTS

Introduction		2
1.	Chapter 1: Accountability	9
2.	Chapter 2: Foundations	19
3.	Chapter 3: Purpose	29
4.	Chapter 4: Patience	39
5.	Chapter 5: Responsibility	49
6.	Chapter 6: Education	59
7.	Chapter 7: Value	69
8.	Chapter 8: Ambition	77
9.	Chapter 9: Ethics	87
10.	Chapter 10: Assistance	99
11.	Chapter 11: Communication	109
12.	Chapter 12: Engagement	121
13.	Chapter 13: Inspiration	131
14.	Chapter 14: Motivation	141

15.	Chapter 15: Teams	153
16.	Chapter 16: Goals	163
17.	Chapter 17: Challenges	173
18.	Chapter 18: Politics	187
19.	Chapter 19: Failure	199
20.	Chapter 20: Balance	209
	Epilogue	219
	Appendix	222
	Please Leave a Review	224
	About Marc Hill	225

READ BEFORE LEADING

20 ESSENTIAL LEADERSHIP LESSONS TO HELP YOU SUCCEED AND AVOID FAILURE

INTRODUCTION

The sharp vibration of my pager jolted me awake at 2:30 AM—my first emergency call as the newly appointed fire chief. Adrenaline surged through my veins as I leaped out of bed, half-blindly scrambling for my pants and racing downstairs to my truck. No more "what ifs" or "if onlys." This was it—my moment—and I was in charge.

"81 Chief en route," I radioed to dispatch as I tore down the street. But as I drove, doubt started to creep into my mind. Would my command be accepted? Was I ready for this? What if no one listened to me? All my grand plans seemed at risk of going up in smoke.

This emergency call was just the first of many brutal awakenings that would strip away my ego and expose the vast canyon between my knowledge and my leadership abilities. Looking back now, after years in the fire service and with the perspective of hard-earned experience, I can say something I never thought I'd admit:

INTRODUCTION

I completely failed as a fire chief and leader—not a little, but spectacularly.

This book is a truthful, straightforward, and unfiltered exploration of the challenges and struggles I faced in leadership. I'm going to be blunt about my mistakes—how I alienated my team with reckless decisions, didn't communicate, didn't listen to others, and underestimated the resistance to change. You might cringe at some of my bigger f-ups; I certainly do when I look back.

Yet here's the silver lining, the lesson in all of this: these painful choices transformed me into a far better leader than any textbook or mentor could have. Each failure peeled away layers of my ego and bravado, revealing a more authentic and effective approach to leadership. It was a truly transformative journey through the fires of adversity, and I emerged on the other side stronger—maybe with a few more gray hairs—and a more capable person.

Leadership books are a dime a dozen. It's a $20-billion industry, with many of them telling you the same old thing in so many similar ways. I was tired of reading about how all these successful people were such great leaders. No one was telling the real truth. Few were admitting to failures and mistakes. There's a common phrase that says, "In order to lead, you must first be able to lead yourself." I'd argue it's more like, "In order to lead, you must first survive your own bad ideas." To be personally responsible for your actions and knowledge. There is no special formula or million-dollar answer to the question of how to be a great leader. It comes down to some basic, simple principles—ones we'll dive into throughout this book.

So, this is the raw story of my ups and downs, my mistake-laden journey in leadership, and how I navigated these challenges. *Read Before Leading* is about real life. It's a reminder of the foundation true leadership is built upon. In today's fast-paced world, effective leadership requires constant learning and reflection. This book dives into the lessons I've learned through failures and mistakes, revealing how they can sharpen your skills and broaden your perspective. Each chapter is a conversation, drawing from my personal stories and insights that highlight the power of hindsight. As you turn these pages, you'll see leadership isn't just about making decisions; it's about making informed choices that resonate with your team and put them first and foremost.

So buckle up—it's going to be a bumpy but informative ride.

Chapter 1: ~~Concerns~~ Accountability

"ONLY THOSE WHO DARE
TO FAIL GREATLY CAN EVER
ACHIEVE GREATLY."

— ROBERT F. KENNEDY

May 22nd, 2014

The village boardroom felt suffocating. The fluorescent lights buzzed overhead, a constant and annoying reminder of where I was and why. I shifted positions in the hard plastic chair, my uniform tightening around me as if it were a straightjacket. Maybe it was my nerves, or maybe it was the crushing weight of what was about to happen.

I looked up at the clock: 6:08 PM. Already eight minutes late. The dread was growing, and every passing second stretched into eternity. I could still barely believe why I was summoned.

At last, the doors behind me opened with an ominous creak. Five board members filed in; their faces were a mix of disappointment, anger, and – worst of all – pity. I straightened my back, squaring my shoulders. I might be on the chopping block, but I won't show weakness. Not now, not after everything.

"Chief Hill," the PFC (Police and Fire Commission) Chairman began, his voice gruff and distant, as though he'd rather

CHAPTER 1: ACCOUNTABILITY

be anywhere else. "We've called this meeting to address some concerns brought to our attention."

As he spoke, my mind began to wander. How did I get here? How did it all come to this? It felt like yesterday I was accepting this job, all smiles and handshakes, eager to show the world what I was made of and prove I was chosen for the right reasons. But leadership isn't about the handshakes or the title. It's about accountability—taking responsibility for both success and failure. And on this day, I was being reminded of that truth in the hardest way possible.

***

Ten short months ago, I was welcomed as the first full-time Fire Chief in Rothschild history. The village had decided they needed a full-time fire and EMS (Emergency Medical Services) chief to coordinate and administer the department of roughly thirty volunteers, part-time, and paid per-call staff. This was going to be a huge change, and no one had planned out effectively. There was an air of disconnect between the village administration and the fire department command staff. You could feel the tension when both parties were in the same room. One group appeared to distrust the other, and because of this, I believe, I was hired from the outside. So welcome Chief Marc Hill to the scene.

I walked into my new office – well, "closet" might be a better word. It was, in fact, a storage closet converted into an office.

Barely big enough for a desk and chair. But it was mine, and I was going to make the most of it.

I sat down in my battered, beaten industrial office chair. Its worn rusted edges hinted at the history I was about to confront. "Alright," I thought, a grin spreading across my face, "let's get this party started." I reached up and pulled out the first dusty binder from the shelf above me, eager to dive head-first into the department's guidelines and procedures.

I wish I had known then just how crazy and unbelievable this ride would turn out to be. If only I'd understood the importance of accountability from day one—not just for others, but for myself. If I had taken a moment to breathe, listen, and understand before charging ahead recklessly, things might have turned out different.

***

"Chief Hill?" the chairman's voice brought me crashing back to reality. Right. The board meeting. The complaints and the mess I'd made.

I cleared my throat, trying to summon the courage to speak. "Yes. I'm aware there have been some... issues and complaints." Understatement of the year right there. Even the words tasted sour and reminded me of my failures.

The chairman sat back and raised an eyebrow, his expression showing a mix of disbelief and disappointment. "Issues?

CHAPTER 1: ACCOUNTABILITY

That's putting it a bit lightly. We've received formal complaints from your entire command staff. They're using words like 'hostile work environment' and 'abuse of power.' Do you care to explain?"

"Nope, but I guess I'm going to have to," I thought.

I opened my mouth, ready to defend myself, to explain how I was just trying to drag this department into the 21st century. But as I looked around the room, at the faces of the board members who had put their trust in me, I felt the fight drain out of me. They weren't interested in excuses or explanations. They wanted accountability.

For the first time, I saw the damage I'd done outside the department. It wasn't just about updating the fire department or getting new equipment. It was about the people – the people I was supposed to lead and support. People I had let down in my rush to prove myself as a leader.

I thought back to some of my first big changes – updating the response protocols. It seemed simple on paper: more efficient and safer for everyone. But I didn't bother to teach it properly and didn't take the time to get buy-in from the team. I was so consumed and focused on the destination I forgot to bring my people along for the ride.

I remembered the look on the Assistant Chief's face when I shot down his concerns. His eyes, usually bright with enthusiasm, had dimmed, and his face barely contained his frustration. "With all due respect, Chief," he said, his lips twitching slightly, "we've been doing it this way for 30 years."

And what did I say? Oh, nothing too bad: "Well, just because you've been doing it that way for 30 years doesn't mean you've been doing it right. Maybe it's high time to teach an old dog new tricks." Wow, real smooth, Marc. Real smooth.

From there, it was a snowball rolling downhill, growing bigger and more destructive. Every change I pushed through, every suggestion I ignored, every time I pulled rank instead of listening – it all led to this moment. This meeting of reckoning.

I looked the board members in the eye and swallowed my pride. "I screwed things up," I said, the words feeling like total defeat. "I came in here thinking I knew everything, I could just force change, and everyone would fall in line. I was totally wrong."

The room fell silent. You could've heard a pin drop – or in this case, the sound of my career falling to the floor. The silence stretched on as the board looked at each other.

The chairman leaned forward, studying me. His expression, which had been hard and unforgiving, softened just a bit. "Well," he said after what felt like forever, "at least you can admit it. That's a start."

A start. Not an end. Maybe there was hope yet. I took a deep breath. I might have fallen, but I wasn't out yet.

"We want you to talk to all your command staff individually.

CHAPTER 1: ACCOUNTABILITY

Get them on the same page," his tone leaving no room for argument. "We'll meet again next month to see how things are coming along," he added.

As I left the boardroom, my head was spinning and my future was uncertain, I realized something. This moment of failure, of humiliation – this was where my real education in leadership began. Sometimes we get caught up in the details, the tunnel vision, and lose sight of the real problem. As they say, the road to Hell is paved with good intentions, and I had the best. But a leader isn't defined by how they handle success. They're defined by how they handle failure—and how they hold themselves accountable when things go wrong.

The PFC gave me a stack of letters, the concerns, that were raised about me. They were eye-opening to say the least. Every member of my command staff had written how I had mismanaged and was seen as a toxic leader. Each letter was a mirror, reflecting the mistakes I had made and the trust I had broken. They were humbling to read. Those letters taught me that being accountable isn't just admitting you're wrong. It's about taking ownership of the impact your decisions have on others.

What Accountability Means

If you ever get called into a meeting like this one, and I hope you never do, take a step back and breathe. Maybe two breaths if necessary. Reflect on what you did and what has happened. You have two choices: defend yourself, or take responsibility. It's tempting to defend and to justify your actions. But real leadership requires accountability. It requires owning your mistakes, reflecting on your actions, and committing to do better. They are the uncomfortable truths you've overlooked or ignored. Clues and signs something is wrong, and a red flag has been raised. Take a moment to pause and reflect on the problems or what the issues might be and why you took the action you did.

I didn't understand this at the time until the end of the meeting. I walked in confident and even a bit arrogant, believing in my choices and stance. But as I sat there, faced with disappointment in the room, I felt my confidence waver. I thought the resistance, the struggles, and the obstacles I faced were just things to be swept aside in the name of my righteous progress. But they weren't. They should've been stoplights on the road, but I chose to run those red lights. And just like running real stoplights, it wasn't long before there was a crash. If I had valued accountability from the start—I could have avoided much of the damage. But as the saying goes, better late than never.

Hindsight is powerful—it gives us the chance to reflect and see the outcomes of our decisions. Sometimes those outcomes are positive; other times, they're far from it. Obviously, if you get a meeting like this, things didn't work out the way you'd planned. Accountability is uncomfortable, but it's also powerful. It's not about being perfect. It's about being real, being honest, and taking responsibility for the choices you make. When you do that, you earn the respect of those you

CHAPTER 1: ACCOUNTABILITY

lead. You build a foundation for success—not just for yourself, but for your entire team.

I initially titled this chapter: Concerns. It wasn't until after the twelfth edit that I thought to myself, "Why concerns? Why am I still trying to defend my actions?" This story is the culmination of my accountability as a leader. The hard truth when I was brought to the carpet to answer for my actions. It had nothing to do with the concerns of the board or of my staff. It was about my leadership failures and the humbling experience when I was forced to be held to account for all of my actions.

As they say in order to lead you must first be able to lead yourself. So I start this book with accountability. Be accountable to yourself and earn the respect of your team by showing them how important it is. That's where true leadership begins.

Lessons Learned:

1. Failures are opportunities for growth and improvement.

2. Be accountable for what you have done and what you have failed to do.

3. Sometimes the end is a new the beginning.

CHAPTER 2:
FOUNDATIONS

"SUCCESS IS THE RESULT OF PERFECTION, HARD WORK, LEARNING FROM FAILURE, LOYALTY, AND PERSISTENCE, ALL BUILT ON A SOLID FOUNDATION."

— GEN. COLIN POWELL

CHAPTER 2: FOUNDATIONS

Pisa, Italy, is home to one of the most iconic towers in the world. The majestic Leaning Tower of Pisa is over 183 feet tall; its marble blocks shine in the sun as it dangerously tilts at 3.97 degrees. This architectural marvel stands nearly 13 feet off its vertical center, but this isn't just a tourist attraction—it's a vital lesson in the importance of solid foundations.

So, why does this 12th-century tower lean anyway? The answer lies hidden beneath the surface, in the soft, unstable soil that can't support the tower's height and weight. With a 9-foot foundation, the tower began to lean even as it was being built. In a show of ingenuity—or perhaps stubbornness—the builders didn't stop construction. Instead, they attempted to correct the tilt by adding counterweights as they went higher, a band-aid solution that eventually proved pointless and only slowed the leaning.

Today, the Leaning Tower of Pisa stands as a witness to the dangers of overlooking the importance of a strong foundation. It's a lesson that extends far beyond architecture, reaching into the heart of leadership.

Over-Eager Leadership

Just as in architecture, building anything of lasting value in life—be it a career, a team, or an organization—requires patience, meticulous planning, and, above all, a rock-solid foundation. As a leader, the responsibility falls on you to lay this groundwork, the bedrock upon which your legacy will be built.

I learned this lesson the hard way. When I began my role as Chief, I made the critical mistake of neglecting this crucial step. Instead of carefully laying a solid foundation, I metaphorically took a fire hose, shoved it into the ground, and turned it on full blast, creating a soupy quicksand that ultimately consumed me and what I was trying to achieve.

My eagerness to make immediate and rushed changes blinded me to the importance of understanding the existing structure. I implemented new policies without fully grasping the department's culture. I reorganized teams without appreciating the intricate web of relationships that had developed over the years. I set ambitious goals without realizing the limitations of our resources.

The result of my over-eagerness? Every decision I made, and every change I implemented, started to crack and pull apart because I failed to establish a proper foundation from the start. Team morale plummeted, productivity suffered, and the improvements I sought to make ended up creating more problems than they solved.

CHAPTER 2: FOUNDATIONS

Building a Solid Foundation

Building a strong foundation as a leader requires patience, planning, and a thorough understanding of the environment you're entering. Just as engineers must consider soil conditions, height, and weight when constructing a building, leaders must assess the organizational culture, resources, and challenges before implementing changes.

Before you start demolition day and rip the walls down to their studs, calculate what you need first. Create a list of needed changes, remodeling, or additions. Investigate what type of foundation you are starting with and what shape it's in. Calculate how large a building you need to construct first and what supplies you need. There is time to figure things out; have patience and start slowly. Investigate, include your team in the process, and ask questions.

Understanding Your Limits and Capabilities

As a leader, it's crucial to understand your limits and capabilities. We all have hopes and desires, and we all make mistakes and fail. That's part of life and the learning process. But how can you gauge your success or even your failure if you don't fully understand what's being asked of you?

Don't fear asking important questions. Instead, fear the lack of answers or an unwillingness to provide them. Remember, you have the power to decline a position if it doesn't feel right. If you have doubts about the answers you've received, ask again in a different way. Get clarity. I didn't do this, and I should have. I ignored my instincts, and it cost me dearly. If your heart, head, and gut are telling you something, listen to them. Understand your capabilities and what the skills and needs of your organization are. There are limits to what a leader can achieve in a given day, month, or year. Plan this out as effectively and efficiently as possible.

Building for the Long Haul

A strong foundation can only be built when all the facts and figures have been calculated. Yes, life happens, the world turns, and you will be forced to adapt and change. But your foundation should be robust enough to endure shifting winds and unforeseen circumstances. As a leader, you must envision the long-term impact of your decisions, much like the architects who designed the great cathedrals of Europe, knowing full well they would never see them completed. They were built with a multi-generational vision—what we now call Cathedral Thinking.

I would never expect to live in a tent for thirty years on the Florida coast without considering the possibility of a hurricane. Don't build a tent and expect the world to not hit it with gale-force winds and torrential rains. The foundation you build should be solid enough to weather any storm, just as cathedrals were constructed to endure centuries of change. It must be built upon your core principles and what you want to achieve as a leader, but also strong enough to outlast you, and to continue standing long after you've moved on.

In many ways, your foundation is the beginning of the legacy you will leave behind. As leaders, we need to adopt a Cathedral Mindset—thinking not just of the immediate challenges, but of how our actions today shape the future of the departments and communities we serve. Like those cathedral builders, we are laying the groundwork for something that will stand for generations, even if we don't witness its final form.

The decisions we make, the culture we build, and the resources we secure are all part of creating a legacy to withstand the test of time. Short-term gains might offer quick wins, but true leadership is about laying the bricks for the future, ensuring the structure can evolve and grow with future generations.

Patience in Foundation Building

What I know now is building a solid foundation takes time, patience, and dedication. Just as you have to set pilings, rebar, and wait for concrete to cure, you also have to wait as a leader. If you are the person in charge, it will take time to talk to your new staff and find out about their attitudes and beliefs. To watch them work and see their dedication. To evaluate their protocols and their equipment.

During this foundation-building phase:

1. Conduct one-on-one meetings with your team members to get to know them and understand their perspectives or concerns.

2. Observe daily operations to identify strengths and weaknesses in current processes.

3. Review past performance data and reports to understand historical challenges and successes.

4. Meet with the key stakeholders (movers and shakers) to align your organizational goals.

5. Assess the available resources and identify any gaps that need to be addressed.

Remember, this investment of time upfront will pay dividends in the long run, helping you avoid the pitfalls of over-eager decision-making and ill-timed changes. And, if nothing else, it will give you plenty of material for your own book!

Pisa or the Cathedrals?

The foundation you set will determine your success. I started this book with foundations because it was the base I neglected that affected everything else. Foundations in leadership will affect your integrity, trust, credibility, communication, ethics, value, purpose, and the many other tangible and intangible aspects we will discuss further.

A strong foundation isn't built overnight, but every step you take toward understanding and preparing for your role is a brick in the wall of your leadership legacy. Will you build a tower that stands the test of time, or one that leans towards failure? The foundation you lay today will determine the answer.

Lessons Learned:

1. Build a solid foundation by understanding the existing structure and culture before implementing changes.

2. Take time to investigate, ask questions, and thoroughly plan to ensure lasting success.

3. Understand your own strengths and limitations, and seek clarity before making major decisions.

Chapter 3: Purpose

"THE PURPOSE OF LEADERSHIP IS TO CREATE AN ALIGNMENT OF STRENGTHS IN WAYS THAT MAKE A SYSTEM'S WEAKNESSES IRRELEVANT."

— PETER DRUCKER

CHAPTER 3: PURPOSE

August 5, 2013

My footsteps echoed in the hallway as I paced up and down outside the Village Community Room. I nervously kept glancing down at the key points I'd scribbled on a piece of scrap paper. Hopefully this would be the final interview for Fire Chief. The main door creaked open, and an older gentleman peaked his head out and waved me in, quietly whispering, "Good luck," before shutting the door behind me.

In the middle of the room stood a single chair. As I approached, I couldn't resist a wisecrack to break the tension. "I guess this is the hot seat," I said, settling into the chair as subdued laughter rippled through the room. The Police and Fire Commission (PFC) Board, along with the Village President, sat slightly elevated above me; their expressions were blank and unreadable.

"Welcome back, Marc," the PFC Chairman began. "This will be a short meeting." I braced myself, expecting another round of grueling questions. Instead, he continued, "To get right down to it, we'd like to offer you the job."

I sat in stunned silence for a moment. I had prepared for another interview, not a job offer. All I could manage was a stammering, "Well, thank you."

The Village President gestured his hand across the room towards the fire station. "We've got a lot of hope for you over there." He then leaned forward, pressing his hands together as he met my gaze. His words were simple but loaded with expectation: "We expect you to fix things."

"Fix things. What did that mean?" I thought, but I also never asked for specifics. I assumed it meant one thing: to fix everything I found wrong. Little did they know at the time, but those two words would become another of my many mantras, my mission, and, ultimately, my downfall. But in the moment, I felt a surge of purpose and determination. Those two words resonated in my head they became my "why". They rang out in nearly every action I would undertake going forward. Fix things.

Finding Your Purpose

Purpose is vital in life. Without it, we flounder, stumbling through our days like someone searching for objects in a dark room. We need purpose in our daily mission and in our broader life journey to achieve and strive for something. Finding your purpose can be a pivotal moment, one that fills you with the belief there's a reason for your existence.

Purposeful leadership is a key aspect of how you guide your team. I took the "fix things" mentality to heart, feeling I had been given carte blanche to do as I saw fit. Come hell or high water, I was going to "fix things" and make them better than I found them. Resistance be damned, change was a-comin'!

Purposeful leadership starts with understanding why you're in the role. Why did they hire you? What do they really need from you? In my case, I thought they wanted me to tear everything apart and rebuild it better. But that wasn't the real "why." My purpose should've been to guide, to listen, and to lead—not to bulldoze my way through the department.

Discovering the real purpose in leadership involves a few key steps:

1. **Understand your role.** Your purpose starts with knowing why you're there. It's not always about fixing things; sometimes, it's about improving, supporting, or guiding.

2. **Talk to your team.** I missed this crucial step. I didn't take the time to sit down with everyone and truly listen to their perspectives. Listening gives you insight into the broader purpose—the collective "why" of the team. You can't lead effectively if you don't know what your team stands for.

3. **Align your purpose with theirs.** Your purpose as a leader doesn't have to match the organization's or the team's, but it should be connected. I thought I was there to fix everything. The team, on the other hand, was focused on serving the community and main-

taining stability. If I had understood that, I could've found a balance between my desire for change and their need for continuity.

4. **Communicate your purpose.** Once you've found your "why," share it with the team. Don't leave it to interpretation. Clear communication ensures everyone is moving in the same direction.

Purpose as a Leader vs. Purpose as a Team

Your purpose as a leader can—and often will—be more focused than the broader purpose of the team. In my case, my purpose was centered around fixing what I saw as broken. But the team's purpose was about community service. These purposes weren't mutually exclusive, but I didn't recognize that at the time. If I had, I could've worked to align my vision for change with their commitment to serving the public.

The lesson here is that your purpose doesn't have to define the whole team. But it should complement and enhance the collective mission. Your role is to help the team discover their own purpose and align it with the organization's broader goals. This builds unity and trust, two key elements of successful leadership.

The problem I ran into was not seeing this difference. I pushed for what I thought was right, not realizing the team wasn't aligned with my specific goal. Had I recognized it, we could have found a way to move forward together—balancing my desire for change with their need for stability.

The Importance of Perspective

Your perspective in the leadership position will also determine your purpose. I looked at the Fire Chief position I was in as a construction worker remodeling a home. My mentality was to relish in the demolition of the old ways and celebrate the new. I failed to understand many people were living in the home and liked it just as it was. Every time I took the metaphorical sledgehammer to the drywall and pulled out a fixture, they were disgusted.

Perspective has everything to do with how you choose to look at things. As a leader, you need to accept this fact and understand it. Just because you see a problem does not mean others will. It is your job to articulate what you see and why you would change it. How you go about communicating your perspective will directly impact your success or your failure.

The Power of Purpose

Purpose will drive you. Purpose will push you. Purpose will give you clarity and confidence. But make sure your purpose is the right one, and not constantly recalculating your route over and over.

Have confidence in what you say and in what you want to achieve. When you are a confident leader, you will be far more likely to be respected. Your purpose will feed your fire to embrace the ability to take and make decisive actions. Having confidence will empower you to stand firm, even when you face doubt and setbacks. Purpose will fuel your belief in your ability to achieve your goals and inspire others to follow your lead.

I lacked the humility to question my purpose or adapt it when things weren't working. Instead, I clung to my belief that "fixing things" was the only path forward. That's not leadership; that's stubbornness. Don't make that mistake. Embrace your purpose with confidence. After all, if you can't believe in yourself, who will? Take the time to be patient, humble, and put in the hard work to communicate the purpose you have with everyone.

By combining purpose with confidence, you'll refine your direction and boost your leadership ability. Confidence transforms purpose from a simple idea into a driving force to propel you toward your goals and inspire those around you.

Turning Purpose into a Vision

Once you've nailed down your purpose, the next step is figuring out how to turn it into a vision. Purpose gives you your "why"—the foundation for everything you do. But vision? Vision is where you're headed, your destination. Most departments or organizations have a mission statement that covers the basics—what they do and why. But a vision goes deeper. It's long-term. It's where you want to take that purpose and how it will shape the future.

As a leader, you have to understand how these two ideas connect. Purpose gives you a broad direction, but vision sharpens your focus. Vision is the result of refining your purpose, of asking yourself: What will this look like down the road? What impact will it have, and how will I know when we've made it? Like building a Cathedral!

Looking back, I missed a key piece of this puzzle. My vision was all about me—what I wanted to accomplish, what I thought was best. I ignored the importance of "we." The real vision should've included my team and their role in shaping a new future. "We" always goes further than "I." But I didn't share my purpose clearly, and I didn't invite my team to help shape the vision. If I had, I could've built something lasting, something real. A vision to inspire everyone, not just me.

Purpose isn't just a motivational buzzword—it's the foundation of leadership. It's your "why," and it gives you and your team direction. But purpose alone isn't enough. You need a shared vision to turn that purpose into action, and you need to communicate that vision clearly to everyone involved.

Lessons Learned:

1. Avoid taking directions at face value without understanding their deeper meaning.

2. Make sure your purpose is communicated to your team and aligns with their values and goals.

3. Purposeful leadership is a shared journey, not a solitary path.

CHAPTER 4: PATIENCE

"PATIENCE IS BITTER,
BUT ITS FRUIT IS SWEET."

— ARISTOTLE

CHAPTER 4: PATIENCE

Charlie was a probationary firefighter, fresh out of the training academy, overflowing with energy and enthusiasm. He's got a look in his eye, the one that says, "I'm ready to take on the world." We've all seen it before. Hell, I had the same look when I first started.

One day, we get a call for a working house fire. As the engine company rolls up, Charlie's practically jumping out of his skin, ready to charge in. He's nearly reaching for the hose before the truck even stops. But Mike, a veteran of 25 years, calm as ever, just puts a hand on the rookie's shoulder and says, "Wait, just wait."

Charlie gives him a look, like, "Are you kidding me? We don't have time to wait!" But the veteran doesn't flinch. He just stands there, scanning the scene as he's preparing his SCBA (Self-Contained Breathing Apparatus). He's watching the fire and the smoke, listening to it like it's talking to him. The rookie is practically vibrating with impatience, but he reluctantly waits.

After a few seconds, the veteran nods to the Lieutenant as he points to the side door. "We're going in," he says, but not through the front like the rookie wanted. They moved to a side door, away from where the flames are licking at the front door.

They go in, handle the fire, and as they're pulling out, the roof over the front door collapses. If they'd gone in the way the rookie wanted, they'd be trapped under rubble. The rookie doesn't say anything, but you can see it in his eyes—the realization, the understanding.

Patience isn't about sitting around, twiddling your thumbs. It's about knowing when to act and when to wait. The rookie thought speed was everything, but the veteran and the officer knew better. In the heat of the moment, pause an extra second to take in the full picture. Having patience can keep you alive.

That's the lesson you can't teach in a classroom. You only learn it when you've been in the thick of it enough times to know sometimes, the best thing you can do is just... wait.

Patience is a virtue. At least, that's what is commonly said. But why are some virtues so hard to practice and master? If they are aspects of a person's character that make them a moral and good person, then it should be easy to accomplish, right? Patience, on the other hand, is one I have found to be challenging to grasp.

The Humility of Patience

Every morning, as I walked to my office, I'd repeat the same phrase to myself like a mantra: "There's no time like the

CHAPTER 4: PATIENCE

present." I convinced myself every second spent thinking and not acting was a second wasted. Action was everything. If I didn't move fast, I'd lose momentum. And that's how I justified the whirlwind of changes I threw at the department. The village PFC had one directive for me: "Fix things." So, I fixed things fast.

But fast fixes have a way of falling apart, don't they? I didn't see this at the time. I thought I was doing what needed to be done, charging ahead, leading from the front. I was the example, wasn't I? I didn't stop to realize patience wasn't passivity. It wasn't about sitting back and doing nothing. Patience is active. It's hard. It's looking at the whole picture instead of just your narrow view of it.

I was too wrapped up in my head and my ideas to do that. I thought I had to prove myself by moving quickly and by making things happen. But what I didn't understand was real leadership, the kind that stands the test of time, isn't about forcing things into place. It's about understanding change takes time, and people need to be brought along with you, not dragged behind kicking and screaming.

And patience? Patience is about humility. It's knowing you don't have all the answers, and you don't have to. It's the ability to step back and let things unfold when necessary, to listen more than you speak, and to realize other people's perspectives matter. Patience forces us to remain grounded in the work we are trying to do, to stay humble, and realize the importance doesn't lie with us but with those we are trying to serve and lead.

The Downfall of Impatience

Unfortunately, not having much patience is a character flaw of mine. I've always been the guy who just couldn't sit still. If something needed doing, I had to do it right then and there. Waiting around felt like wasting time, and wasting time was the last thing I wanted. The compliments I'd hear didn't help either. "Marc's a man of action." "Need something done? Ask Marc." My ego swelled with pride each time I heard it, making me feel as if I could do no wrong.

So, when I landed the chief leadership role, I had something to prove to everyone, but mostly to myself. I threw myself into the work, charging ahead like I could single-handedly transform the entire department. I was ready to show the world I wasn't just here to fill a position; I was here to lead.

But I got ahead of myself. No, scratch that—I sprinted ahead of myself. I rewrote the Standard Operating Guidelines (SOGs) faster than you could blink. Printed them up, slapped them into binders, and handed them off to the officers. "Take a look, let me know what you think," I said, already mentally patting myself on the back for getting it done so quickly.

I didn't notice the looks I got, those half-raised eyebrows, the silent hesitation. I didn't stop to ask if they understood the changes or if they even agreed with them. I was too busy moving on to the next hurdle. In my head, I'd already checked that task off the list.

But that's where I screwed up. There was no buy-in, no conversation. I didn't give them time to digest the changes, let alone introduce them to the crews. I was so focused on showing everyone I could get things done, I missed the most important part: ensuring what I was doing worked.

Patience? I shoved it to the side like it was some outdated relic. I was too busy taking immediate action, too caught up in the rush of "getting things done." And that overinflated sense of self? Yeah, it blinded me. E-G-O spells stupidity, and I was swimming in it.

My overinflated ego pushed aside the most important factors that would have ensured success. My impatience and real lack of respect for others' opinions and ideas alienated everyone from what I was trying to achieve. Work smarter and work efficiently, but work with your team.

The Essence of True Change

Changes take time to see through. This is especially true when you're the new leader. Don't bite off more than you can chew. You can eat an elephant, but it takes one bite at a time. These are all old sayings, but they all ring true. When you walk into a new environment, the changes you want to make, or think should be made, will take time to achieve. You might see items you want to change, but if you wait, you will find out there may be a reason for them to be done a certain way. Never assume you know anything or everything—this is especially true when you are coming in from the outside or from someplace new.

Instead of rushing in, I should've started slowly by making observations and keeping a written record of what I saw. Organize your thoughts and beliefs. Write down the issues and challenges you see, and address them with your team. Investigate the why first to get to the how. You have to have the patience to understand the full meaning, and patience takes time.

Change is something we love but also love to hate. It's a process that can make or break your leadership abilities. If you want to make lasting change, it will be a process that is painful and laborious, but most of all, it takes patience. But the finished results will amaze you and those you serve.

Patience is more than just waiting and taking your time to accomplish a task. The Merriam-Webster Dictionary defines patience as:

The capacity to accept or tolerate delay, trouble, or suffering without getting angry or upset.

The common thread is the ability to overcome suffering or struggle. It's debilitating sometimes to be patient and wait. As a leader, we have to master the ability to take a step back and allow time to move. For those of us who are type-A personalities, this waiting is painful. We want to act, to achieve, to fix, and to right the wrong we see in front of us.

Knowing When to Act

Being patient is a hard thing to do because it means we must watch events play out that we may know the likely result of. Having patience as a leader is more about knowing when to act than how to act. Through experience, we learn sometimes the best thing to do is nothing. Sometimes the right thing is to not say anything. And sometimes, if we act immediately to remedy a problem, it takes away the learning opportunity for someone else.

Consider that patience is sometimes more important as a leader than blindly acting. Your team needs to see you listen to the problems and not just shoot from the hip. Sure, sometimes we must take immediate action, especially in the fire service when lives are on the line and time matters. But in most cases, outside a live scene, this is not the case—especially at the higher levels of leadership and management.

You have the time to think. You have the time to plan. You have the time to process and investigate. Use the time to your benefit. Patience will take a great deal of discipline. Set yourself and your team up for success. Don't just rip bandages off and break wounds open again. Take a breath, step back, and look at what is in front of you.

Patience isn't a weakness but a strength. It's a large part of the foundation upon which lasting change is built. It allows for collaboration, understanding, and buy-in from your team. It gives you the time to understand the challenges you face and develop realistic solutions.

As leaders, we must remember our role isn't to make changes but to guide our teams through change. This requires patience, empathy, and a willingness to listen and learn. It's about creating an environment where change is embraced, not forced. It's about building trust and respect, which can only happen over time.

So, to all the leaders out there, chomping at the bit to make their mark: take a deep breath. Slow down. Listen. Observe. Understand. And then, with patience and purpose, lead your team toward positive change. The results may not be immediate, but they will be lasting and meaningful. And isn't that what true leadership is all about? Aristotle's quote is terrific here: patience is bitter and hard to swallow, but the fruit of patience is sweet and can yield great results.

Lessons Learned:

1. Take the time to assess, plan, and seek opinions before you act.

2. Patience allows for deeper, more lasting solutions that will contribute to your foundation.

3. Embrace patience as a strength.

Chapter 5:
Responsibility

"YOU MUST TAKE PERSONAL RESPONSIBILITY. YOU CANNOT CHANGE THE CIRCUMSTANCES, THE SEASONS, OR THE WIND, BUT YOU CAN CHANGE YOURSELF. THAT IS SOMETHING YOU HAVE CHARGE OF."

— JIM ROHN

CHAPTER 5: RESPONSIBILITY

July 29, 2013

As I approached the fire station for my first interview, I saw a small concrete brick building in the shape of a rectangle, with four sun-faded maroon doors that had once been red. It was a simple and spartan structure, built in the late 1940s, now too small for the growing village's needs. But the building's size wasn't the most important detail I should have noticed that day.

Just inside the main entrance, a large black bunting bow lay in the corner of the garage floor. This was a stark reminder of a recent, painful loss. It should have been my first wake-up call. The previous fire chief had passed away just a year prior, after an EMS (Emergency Medical Services) call, leaving the department and community in shock. He had been a beloved figure, rising through the ranks over decades of service.

The black bunting (traditionally used during line-of-duty death funerals) spoke volumes about the pain and grief still present in the station. I should have paid more attention to this. It should have signaled the department was still in mourning and considerable challenges awaited. But I failed to recognize this; instead, I was stubborn and clueless. I saw the bunting and just walked right on by. Because we all know, if we ignore something, it will just go away naturally... right?

As the tour continued, I met some of the on-duty staff. They did their best to be positive and put on happy faces, but I could sense their unease. I was the outsider, the embodiment of impending change. Looking back, it's amazing I never had much doubt about taking the job. None of the warning signs fazed me at all. My ego pushed me to think there was no place to go but up. I didn't open my eyes to truly see what was in front of me and the great responsibility that awaited.

The Weight of Responsibility

I knew, going in as the first full-time fire chief, there would be some natural resistance and animosity, especially as an outsider. However, I didn't fully grasp the weight of responsibility that came with the position. Responsibility, in any leadership role, comes down to the safety of your staff and your ability to give them what they need to grow and thrive. You are the sole person, the leader, who needs to ensure everyone goes home safely and in one piece. This idea isn't just a simple phrase, but should be part of your leadership core values.

Your responsibility is to ensure your team can do their jobs effectively and safely. This is achieved through training and education. The balance of your vision should never put the safety of your staff before the mission. In emergency services, we know our decisions may cost the ultimate price but we put ourselves in direct danger to save lives anyway. However, it's our job as leaders not to put people in danger due to a lack of knowledge, training, or experience.

It's a delicate balance. We can never know everything, and hindsight is 20/20. We need to have the wisdom to recognize our faults, shortcomings, and knowledge gaps. We must strive to remedy these issues and surround ourselves with others who can contribute. Listen to their thoughts and opinions, then make the best decision. This is the balance you need to understand, and you are responsible for finding it.

Being the Problem Solver

One of the big responsibilities of a leader is to be a problem solver or, at the very least, a solution seeker. I used to think I had to solve every problem and issue I found, and that I was the only one who could do so. Because, obviously, the world was waiting for me to come along and fix everything... right?

My responsibility as a leader wasn't to fix everything, but to help my staff see the value in finding their own solutions or guiding them toward those solutions. Micromanagers and control freaks are the types of people who think everything has to be done their way. They lack the confidence and knowledge to understand there are different ways to solve problems. They fear if someone knows more than them, they will be seen as somehow lesser or unworthy. I felt this to a degree. My ego pushed me to think I was the savior, and I had the right ability to lead. Don't think this way. Not only is it unhealthy, but it also will lead to a toxic leadership structure.

As a leader, it's your responsibility to solve problems or at the least find workable solutions. Have the confidence and humility to share the problem with your team. Invite opinions and discussion on the possible solutions. Brainstorm ways to get to the answer with everyone. No one's ever complained about too many good ideas. You'll be amazed at what new thinking and new concepts will blossom. Your responsibility is to have an open eye, ear, and mind. Empower your team to contribute their ideas and expertise. By doing so, you'll not only find better solutions, but also create a more engaged and effective team. Remember, true leadership isn't about having all the answers, but about creating an environment where the best solutions can emerge from the collective wisdom and experience of the group.

The Danger of Assumptions

In my eagerness to make changes, I made a critical mistake. I assumed the responsibility but I didn't understand it. You know the saying, when you assume, you make an ass out of u and me? I was not just responsible for everything that happened in the department, but I was also ultimately responsible for the attitudes, beliefs, actions, and working environment. I took all the negative thinking and feelings of one group and transposed them onto the other without taking a minute to find out the truth for myself. I assumed I knew best. My ego clouded my judgment and gave me tunnel vision. I looked for problems and issues and found them everywhere.

This concept is called confirmation bias or a self-fulfilling prophecy. It can cloud your judgment and directly influence your attitudes, actions, and beliefs. The sad reality is, this feeling is so strong, you often don't realize what went wrong until it's too late. This was my case. I listened to all the naysayers and did not look for the opposite point of view. The hard fact is, the negatives I was hearing reinforced my prior beliefs. They pumped up my inflated ego and my thinking that I was the one who could make the necessary changes. As a leader, you are responsible for looking at all perspectives and evaluating them based on their merits.

You simply cannot go into any situation with this assumptive attitude. You're responsible for researching all points of view first. Talk to people both inside and outside the organization. Once you have all the parts of the puzzle, you can start to put things together in the right order. Remember: no one ever completed a jigsaw puzzle by staring at just one piece. Don't jump to conclusions, and don't believe everything you hear. Never assume.

The Path to True Responsibility

The responsibilities of a leader carry more weight than a person realizes before they earn that role. I thought I knew what it meant to lead. I thought I knew what my job was all about. I thought I had all the skills, knowledge, and abilities to be a success. Boy was I wrong.

Looking back, had I opened my eyes that first day - had I recognized the emotional significance of black bunting and the state of the department - I would've approached my responsibilities differently. I should've taken more time to understand the situation, to heal, and to build trust before pushing for sweeping big changes. I misread the situation because of my blinders I had on and everyone suffered because I didn't understand the responsibility of the position at the time.

Leadership is not about having all the answers or being the lone hero who fixes everything. It's about responsibility - to your team, to your mission, and to yourself. It's about opening your eyes to the realities around you, good and bad, and navigating through them with wisdom, empathy, and integrity.

Remember to open your eyes and ears. Don't just see what you want to see, but avoid tunnel vision by seeing what is truly there. Listen not just to confirm your beliefs or for your turn to preach, but to understand different perspectives and attitudes. And most importantly, take responsibility not just for the changes you want to make, but for the people you're leading through those changes. That is the true essence of responsible leadership.

Lessons Learned:

1. Keep your eyes and ears open. You never know what you will hear or see.

2. Never assume and always look for different perspectives and opinions.

3. Leaders are responsible for all actions their teams make, so ensure they are done properly.

Chapter 6: Education

"AN INVESTMENT IN KNOWLEDGE PAYS THE BEST INTEREST."

— BENJAMIN FRANKLIN

CHAPTER 6: EDUCATION

I took training and education for granted. It's embarrassing to admit, but I thought I had it all figured out. I'd been a teacher, an instructor for years, and I have a master's in educational leadership. I should've been the subject matter expert. Yet, the one area I should have excelled in—the area I could've truly transformed the department—I ignored it. Shocking move, I know.

Looking back, I wasted a golden opportunity. I should've used my skills and knowledge to elevate everyone around me. I could've driven real change through training and education, brought the team to the next level, celebrated their growth, and shifted the entire culture toward improvement. But what did I do instead? I let it sit on the back burner, assuming other priorities were more pressing.

Education is vitally important. A leader has to be a great teacher. No matter what you're trying to achieve, those same core skills—communicating, instructing, inspiring—are all parts of a successful leader. And your education program? It's the backbone of your success. But it's not just about having a perfect program; it's about understanding your role in shaping it and how you can influence it in a positive and meaningful way.

One great example is U.S. General Matthew Ridgway during the Korean War. He took control of an 8th Army, which was exhausted, freezing, and beaten down by months of retreat and defeat. But when Ridgway showed up, he didn't come charging in with new tactics or strategies. He brought common sense and reminded them to remember their basics. He walked through the camp, asked simple questions, refreshed the men on their training, and reinforced the fundamentals. No drastic changes—just a return to the basics they had forgotten or overlooked.

Within weeks, that same army started to believe in themselves again. They turned things around, not with new ideas, but by reapplying what they already knew. Ridgway's genius wasn't about innovation; it was about helping his soldiers remember what worked in the first place.

It's a lesson I wish I'd learned sooner.

As a leader, sometimes the best thing you can do is not reinvent the wheel, but refine it. Go back to the fundamentals. Make sure your team is using their knowledge, skills, abilities, and most importantly, they believe in them.

My Not-So-Great Idea

The department had a long-established weekly training session every Monday night from 6 PM to 9 PM, covering various topics such as firefighting, EMS, and rescue operations. The program was well-attended and had participation from all members. It was a system that worked—but I saw room for improvement.

In my eagerness to implement change, I made a critical mistake. Instead of building upon the existing foundation, I dismantled the entire training and education system. I replaced it with a mandatory check-off session for both EMS and fire operations, requiring every member to pass "my checkoffs" to continue serving. I put everyone through Marc's evaluation system, which needed my seal of approval. Instead of building and growing, I started fires where they didn't belong.

However well-meaning my intentions were—I wanted to raise the bar and show my commitment to excellence—but my approach was all wrong. I discarded what was already working, and in the process, alienated people and made more enemies. Instead of recognizing the strengths of the existing program and building on them, I missed the opportunity to improve through training and development. What I should have done was focus on refining the basics and driving consistent growth and improvement. Hell, it was working out just fine; I should've left it alone.

Sometimes in our blind eagerness to change things, we lose sight of what works. Take a moment and step back. Look at what you have before you and find out what is broken or could use a tune-up. Not everything needs to be changed to the way you want it.

The Right Approach

The reaction to my check-offs was immediate and harsh. The veterans felt disrespected—and they had every right to be. I ignored the experience of those who had been part of the department for decades. I let myself fall into the ego trap of thinking I knew better, assuming what they were doing was wrong just because it was different.

That experience was a wake-up call. I learned while education and training are critical, how you implement change is just as important—if not more. Here's what I should've done instead of trying to reinvent the wheel:

1. **Review the system**: Figure out what's working and what isn't.

2. **Acknowledge what works**: Focus on the strengths of the current program.

3. **Remodel, don't bulldoze**: Improve the system instead of scrapping it entirely.

4. **Small tweaks, big impact**: Targeted changes can do more than sweeping overhauls.

5. **Involve the team**: Lean on your veterans and their wealth of experience.

Keep Learning Fun & Interesting

Had I taken a moment to review, reflect, and enhance instead of bulldozing, I would have been able to drive real, lasting change. True leadership embraces the power of education by aligning training with your organizational goals. Training isn't a solo mission. Let your team speak up! Get their input before you start handing out the lecture notes. You'll be surprised how often their concerns mirror your own.

Keep it interesting and engaging. When you approach training as a collaboration rather than a mandate from on high, the improvements become their ideas—not just yours. Before you know it, you're not just the person with the master's degree; you're the leader who guided them to believe they came up with the ideas on their own. To keep things interesting, bring in outside speakers or use your in-house experts. You'd be amazed how many people have a passion or hobby they'd love to share—sometimes the biggest spark comes from the most unexpected places.

And let's be honest—all successful educational programs have a measurement tool or evaluation. You simply must have some way to gauge and assess the level of understanding. This will enable you to set benchmarks and show improvement. On my website, twodarkthirty.com, you'll find a bunch of free lesson plans and tools to help you do just that. Go ahead, steal some ideas.

Lead by example. Share the books you're reading, the classes you're attending, and the conferences you want to check out. Make these opportunities available to your staff as well. When they see you investing in your growth, they'll be more inclined to follow. Be the leader you wish you had.

Finding the Balance

Education and training are indeed the cornerstones of effective leadership and organizational success. However, implementing a strong educational program requires a reasonable approach. It's about recognizing the value in existing systems while having the vision to improve and adapt to them.

As leaders, our role is to create an environment where learning is constant, skills are continuously improved, and every team member feels valued for their knowledge and experience. By building upon the existing foundations, rather than starting from scratch, we can create training programs that use the institutional knowledge and enhance and move it forward.

Remember, the goal of education in leadership is not to showcase your expertise, but to elevate and improve the entire team. When we approach training with this mindset, we create organizations that are highly skilled but also unified in their commitment to excellence. Lift the team up, show them what you do know, and allow them to show you what they know. Together, you will learn from each other.

In the end, true leadership is a mix of education and experience. It's about refining what you've got while guiding your team to grow and excel. And if you can avoid bulldozing the good stuff, you're already ahead of the game.

Lessons Learned:

1. Effective education involves improving existing systems rather than replacing them entirely.

2. Implementing change requires involving the team, respecting their experience, and aligning training with organizational goals.

3. Continuous learning and leading by example create a culture where skills are constantly improved, and the team feels valued and unified.

Chapter 7: Value

"THE VALUE OF LEADERSHIP LIES IN GUIDING OTHERS TO SUCCESS. IN ENSURING THAT EVERYONE IS PERFORMING AT THEIR BEST, DOING THE WORK THEY ARE PLEDGED TO DO, AND DOING IT WELL."

— TRAVIS BRADBERRY

CHAPTER 7: VALUE

I often found myself taking breaks from the mountain of paperwork in my cramped office, leaning back in my chair to listen to the ebb and flow of conversations drifting through the walls. The report room next door was more than just a space with two computer workstations and a couple of worn office chairs; it was the beating heart of the station, where the day shift crew gathered to share their lives.

Sometimes I'd hear laughing; sometimes, I'd hear nothing but the typing of a keyboard.

As a leader, you can feel when something's wrong. You can feel the tension in the air. I'd often experience this as I walked out of my office and into the report room. The talking would stop immediately. People would turn and start to work on one thing or another. The mood would change as soon as I entered. This atmosphere created a wall between us.

I would turn and head back to my office, feeling like a stranger in my own home. Once gone, I could hear the talking start up again. I knew something had to change. At that point, even the printer felt more welcome in the report room than I did. A leader should be part of their team, not separate from it. The disconnect and gap were deeper than just the few steps between my office and the report room—it was a canyon in trust, in understanding, and in how they felt about their place under my leadership.

The crew didn't feel I valued them. They acted differently toward me. As a leader, you do need to have a different relationship with your crew, but animosity and tension should never be part of the equation. I needed to find a way to bridge this gap, to show them I was on their side. But at that moment, sitting alone in my office, the task felt as impossible as putting out a five-alarm fire with a garden hose.

Defining Value in Leadership

Value in leadership is complicated. It's the positive change we bring, the growth we want to nurture, and the purpose we instill in our messaging. It's about making every interaction, every decision, and every initiative count towards something greater than ourselves. When we lead with value at our heart, we transform routine tasks into meaningful roles and turn ordinary teams into extraordinary forces.

The impact of value-driven leadership ripples through an organization in many profound ways. It creates a magnetic culture, which attracts top talent and retains it. In today's ever-changing workplace, especially among the younger generations, there's an intense hunger for value. Employees aren't just looking for a paycheck; they're seeking a sense of meaning and impact in their work. They're looking for a deeper sense of purpose. In emergency services, we're lucky our mission often speaks for itself. But the real question is: do your people know what they're doing makes a difference? How do you show them their efforts contribute to something greater?

Leaders who can tap into this desire for meaning create environments where people thrive. When you make it clear every role, no matter how small, adds value to the larger mission, you ignite a passion, which drives performance, loyalty, and innovation.

Creating Value as a Leader

So, how do we, as leaders, create and spread value? It starts with a shift in perspective. Instead of asking, "What can I gain?" we must ask, "What can I give?" This mindset reframes our approach to leadership, turning it from a position of authority into a platform for service.

Here are some practical strategies to put value into your leadership:

1. **Clarity of Purpose**: Make sure your team understands the "why" behind their work. Help them see how their efforts tie into the larger organizational goals.

2. **Empowerment**: Give people the tools, resources, and freedom they need to make contributions. Trust in their abilities and encourage their growth.

3. **Recognition:** Celebrate the behaviors and outcomes that add value. Recognizing their efforts reinforces the importance of their work but also motivates them to keep pushing forward.

4. **Continuous Learning:** Create an environment where learning and improvement are constant. Encourage curiosity, embrace failures as learning moments, and lead by example in your own growth.

5. **Community Impact:** Find ways for your organization to make a broader impact—whether it's through community outreach, charitable work, or finding solutions to local problems. Your value as a leader grows when you connect your team's efforts to the larger community.

The Legacy of Value

As leaders, the value we add becomes a big part of our legacy. People will forget specific projects or initiatives, but they will always remember how we made them feel and the impact we had on their lives and careers. When we consistently add value, we create a positive ripple effect that extends far beyond our immediate sphere of influence.

Building a legacy of value isn't done overnight. It's the accumulation of countless small actions, moments where you choose to uplift someone, or take a step back to listen. It's showing up every day with the intention to make a positive difference, no matter how small that difference may seem.

True leadership value isn't measured by accolades or titles; it's measured by the growth you inspire in others, the culture you help shape, and the lasting impact you leave behind. When we approach leadership with this in mind, we create organizations, which don't just function—they thrive with or without us.

Make it a habit to ask yourself, "How can I add value today?" Let this question shape your interactions, inform your decisions, and guide your actions. You might even find yourself becoming the person people want to talk to—not just when they need something.

The most effective leaders are the ones who find balance between driving change and valuing what's already working. They create environments where education, experience, and empowerment work hand in hand to create a shared vision. When we lead with this value, we don't just lead successful teams—we build something to last, something that truly makes a difference.

Lessons Learned:

1. Building a strong connection with your team is essential to creating a supportive work environment.

2. Value-driven leadership transforms routine tasks into meaningful roles and creates a sense of purpose and impact within the team.

3. Consistently adding value through clear vision, empowerment, recognition, continuous learning, and community impact creates a lasting legacy.

Chapter 8: Ambition

"KEEP AWAY FROM THOSE WHO TRY TO BELITTLE YOUR AMBITIONS. SMALL PEOPLE ALWAYS DO THAT, BUT THE REALLY GREAT MAKE YOU BELIEVE THAT YOU TOO CAN BECOME GREAT."

— MARK TWAIN

CHAPTER 8: AMBITION

The 80s were a time of money, fame, power, and the lifestyles of the rich and famous. As a kid, I remember watching the movie *Wall Street*. In the iconic film, Gordon Gecko, a shrewd stock market trader, stands before a room of shareholders and confidently declares, "The point is, ladies and gentlemen, that greed, for lack of a better word, is good. Greed is right. Greed works." In the moment, Gecko embodies the raw, unrelenting force of ambition. To him, he sees greed as ambition—a relentless desire for more—drives innovation, competition, and success. He sees it as the fuel behind success. At face value, it's a seductive philosophy, especially in a world that often celebrates winning at all costs.

But here's the dichotomy: ambition, when left unchecked, can quickly change into something darker, as it does for Gecko. As his pursuit of more wealth and power consumes him, he crosses ethical boundaries, betrays those around him, and ultimately faces ruin. What begins as a hunger for success becomes an insatiable thirst. "Greed," in Gecko's world, is no longer just a motivator—it's a blinding obsession that erodes everything in its path.

As leaders, we need to recognize the same duality in our ambition. It has the power to drive us towards achieving greatness, allowing us to establish ambitious objectives and motivate the people we are leading. However, ambition can tempt us to make ethical compromises, leading to actions that contradict our moral values and beliefs. Just as Gordon Gecko, we might begin to think that the ends justify the means - the non-stop quest for success is what counts the most. However, it does not.

The lesson here is ambition, like greed, needs boundaries. Lacking moral values can result in ambition causing destruction. But with purpose and humility, ambition has the potential to serve as a strong motivator, driving us towards our objectives while also uplifting those around us. And let's face it, no one ever says, I'm so inspired by how that guy cheated his way to the top!

In leadership, the challenge isn't to stifle ambition but to channel and use it positively. We need to cultivate the ambition that drives us to be better without losing sight of the bigger picture. True success is more than just winning—it's leaving a legacy built on integrity, trust, and the impact we have on those we lead.

My Journey of Ambition

My journey in leadership has taught me similar lessons about the power and downsides of ambition. I began my career in education, earning a degree to become a teacher and coach.

CHAPTER 8: AMBITION

My ambition was clear: to influence the next generation of youth, to be a positive example, and to show them Social Studies and History could be fun and important subjects. I loved teaching and coaching; I found great fulfillment in the work. It became my passion and my identity.

This ambition served me well. It drove me to excel in my job, to connect with my students, and to continually improve my teaching methods. But ambition, by its nature, is rarely satisfied with the status quo. It grows and wants more.

As time went on, my ambitions shifted. I realized my love had grown to include a desire to become a principal, to be a leader who could drive and influence an entire school. This new goal pushed me to earn my master's degree in educational leadership and begin to act in that new role. I enjoyed budgeting, finding answers for teachers, supporting them, and solving new obstacles. It gave me a new direction.

Here, ambition was my ally. It motivated me to pursue further education, to take on new challenges, and to expand my skill set. Without this drive, I might have remained content in my teaching role, never exploring the broader impact I could have as an administrator.

However, life had other plans. Budget cuts led to me losing my teaching position, and I found myself out of a job, having lost my identity and the drive to continue in the field. It was time to adapt and overcome.

This setback taught me an important lesson about ambition:

I must be flexible. Being too fixed on a particular position or job can make it difficult for us to adapt when situations evolve, resulting in confusion. My ambition is about the desire to grow, to contribute, to make a difference—and these goals can be achieved in many ways.

My time as a volunteer firefighter motivated me to seek a full-time position. In Wisconsin, most fire departments mandate a paramedic license for full-time employment. Obtaining my paramedic certification was extremely challenging and pushed me beyond my comfort zone. However, my drive and enthusiasm to support and impact others remained unchanged. I found new avenues to feed this desire, earning more certifications and gaining experience, which eventually led me to the full-time fire chief role.

This transition showcased the positive power of ambition. It drove me to reinvent myself, to take on new challenges, and to continue growing even when my original career path was no longer viable. Ambition gave me the courage to start over and the perseverance to succeed in a new field.

But ambition, left unchecked, can also lead us astray. I thought I was prepared for the fire chief role, but I was letting my ego and ambition cloud my wisdom and knowledge.

The Dangers of Unchecked Ambition

So, did I fail as a fire chief because of the situation, or did I fail because I did it for the wrong reasons?

CHAPTER 8: AMBITION

This experience made me face the negative aspects of ambition. Occasionally, our ambition to achieve can obscure our boundaries or the truths of a situation. We might go after a job not because we're fully prepared, but because we think we should or because we fear missing out.

The Peter Principle is a popular theory in the field of sociology. It suggests that the most suitable candidate for a position may not always be the immediate successor. The top lieutenant or captain doesn't necessarily need to be the top engineer or driver. The top engineer isn't necessarily the top firefighter, and the top fire chief doesn't have to be the top captain or battalion chief. This is true of any workplace or any job hierarchy.

This principle highlights an important fact regarding ambition: the desire to succeed may not always match our true skills or what the organization requires. At times, ambition drives us to seek positions that may not align with our abilities or experience.

In writing this book and in all of the self-reflection it has caused, I've had to ask myself some tough questions. Did I want to become a fire chief for the right reasons? Was I ready? The answer, and the truth, is no.

I pushed myself because I thought I had to, because I thought as I was getting older, my opportunities were going to dry up, and I needed to jump at the next thing offered. Desperation. I was desperate not to let my family down and to avoid putting any more undue pressure on my wife and kids. I took the fire chief position with a negative gut feeling and apprehension. My ego told me to ignore this and to shut up, but those negative thoughts and energy turned out to be right... or maybe I just fulfilled my dark prophecy.

This is where ambition can become dangerous. When it's fueled by fear, desperation, or ego rather than a genuine desire to contribute and grow, it can lead us to make poor decisions. We might take on roles we're not ready for or pursue paths that don't align with our true values and strengths.

Don't get me wrong, I don't want to scare someone out of the leadership role. Far from it. I had great joy in leading and have found fulfillment in helping others. It's a rewarding experience, and one very few things in life can come close to. But I wanted to write this book to show the world that even when you do make mistakes and fail, there are lessons to be learned. Learn from mine and avoid making the same ones I did.

Ambition and Leadership

How do we harness the positive power of ambition while avoiding its downfall? Here are some key lessons I've learned:

1. **Self-awareness is crucial.** Think about your motivations, strengths, and areas for improvement. Are you pursuing a goal because it truly aligns with your values and abilities, or are you doing it for other reasons?

2. **Embrace continuous learning.** Ambition should drive us to constantly improve and expand our skills, not just to seek higher titles.

3. **Be patient.** Sometimes, the most ambitious thing you can do is to stay in your current role and focus on mastering it completely before moving on.

4. **Seek feedback.** Others often see our strengths and weaknesses more clearly than we do. Regular, honest feedback can help ensure your ambitions are realistic.

5. **Focus on contribution, not just advancement.** Ask yourself how you can best serve your team, organization, or community. Sometimes, this might mean taking a step back rather than pushing for the next rung on the ladder.

6. **Be flexible.** As my journey shows, life doesn't always go as planned. True ambition is about the desire to grow and contribute, not about achieving a specific title or role.

Keep in mind that ambition should be viewed as a tool rather than a goal in itself. When used effectively, it has the potential to motivate us to accomplish significant goals, develop, and create positive change. But like any powerful tool, it should be used with caution, intelligence, and with a defined objective. Let your ambition fuel your growth and desire to contribute, but never let it override your values, integrity, self-awareness, or your commitment to serving others.

Lessons Learned:

1. Flexibility in ambition is crucial; adapting to new paths when circumstances change allows you to continue making a difference.

2. Unchecked ambition, driven by fear or ego, can lead to poor decisions, so ensure your goals align with your true values and strengths.

3. Self-awareness and continuous learning are key; regularly reflect on your motivations, seek feedback, and focus on serving your team and community.

Chapter 9: Ethics

"IN MATTERS OF STYLE,
SWIM WITH THE CURRENT;
IN MATTERS OF PRINCIPLE,
STAND LIKE A ROCK."

— THOMAS JEFFERSON

CHAPTER 9: ETHICS

September 18, 2013

The phone call came three weeks before I was to be sworn in as Fire Chief. At first, it didn't seem unusual—the village clerk, president, and I had been negotiating my salary and benefits. But this call was different. The clerk informed me the board had just approved an early start. The reason? They lacked confidence in the previous month's payroll submission by the acting chief and command staff. They wanted me to investigate potential wrongdoing and fraudulent hourly wage submissions.

I was taken aback. All I could manage was an unenthusiastic, "Um, OK."

That evening, I broke the news to my wife about my earlier start date. As we both looked at each other, a little stunned, I realized what I had just said out loud: fraud and mismanagement. Terrific—this was exactly how I wanted to start.

The next day, I drove into the parking lot at the fire station without fanfare. No door code, no ID, no formal badge pinning, or swearing-in ceremony, and no cake. Just me, knocking on the door, introducing myself to a bewildered firefighter, and asking him to show me to the office.

To say it was awkward would be an understatement. It bordered on ridiculous. I asked the officer in charge (OIC) of the day crew to walk me through the scheduling system and hourly wage calculations. Everything seemed straightforward. During this process, one of the day crew called the assistant chiefs, and they both came to investigate my unexpected early arrival.

As they walked in together, they exchanged a glance, then turned their gaze toward me, eyes narrowing as they tried to size me up. They immediately asked what was going on. It was an uncomfortable moment. I didn't know what to tell them. Do I tell them the truth? Do I lie? I simply said I'd been asked to start early and submit the monthly wages as my first task. It wasn't the whole truth, but it also wasn't a lie. Shades of gray. This was my first ethical choice as a leader.

Uncovering Issues and Missed Opportunities

I should have been more straightforward and honest with them both. There was no need to keep the command staff in the dark. Trust is earned, and I missed an opportunity to begin building trust. As it turned out, after my limited but thorough examination, everything seemed fine. No shady calculations were being made. No fraud was found. But what a way to start.

This story illustrates the deep mistrust that seemed to exist between the village administration and the fire department

CHAPTER 9: ETHICS 91

command. I could see poor communication had led to ingrained negative opinions on both sides. I found myself caught in the middle, asked by the "top" to fix things and push the department forward while facing resistance from the "bottom" as an outsider replacing a beloved chief.

Not asking the right questions or expressing my true feelings set a poor tone for the start of my Fire Chief career. I put myself in a tough spot, digging a hole that was nearly impossible to climb out of. My moral compass pointed one way, but my actions went another.

When you start investigating and asking questions, you often uncover unexpected issues. It's like remodeling a home—you never know what you'll find behind the walls. The big question is: when you see a problem, are you going to walk by it? I find it difficult, if not impossible, to ignore issues. It's a character trait that can be both a strength and a weakness.

As I settled into my new role, I discovered numerous other issues. The department was behind on required testing for essential equipment like SCBA bottles, hoses, ropes, and ladders. Some frontline gear was decades out of date. We still had brass couplings on hoses from the 1970s mixed in with new aluminum hose couplings (a technical no-no).

The bigger issue wasn't with the investigations or replacing outdated materials. Where I went wrong was in how I handled the situation. Despite my background as a teacher, I missed the chance to educate and lift everyone up. Instead, I acted on assumptions, feeding into my ego and the belief that those around me weren't up to the task, and only I could solve the problem alone.

When you find ethical issues and challenges, you should address them. Don't ignore them, as they often grow worse over time. However, the way you go about fixing these problems is entirely within your control. You don't have to do it all by yourself. Ask for help. Find out if anyone else has an interest in helping you remedy the situation. Maybe this is a teaching opportunity?

I should have started outlining the issues and challenges and then focused on educating and uniting the team. Forming committees or groups to divide the workload and share responsibility would have made a huge difference. Involving others will take time and patience, but it will be well worth your efforts. It's a chance to build a stronger team and create a safer environment that prioritizes everyone's best interests.

Balancing Ethics with Confident Humility

When it comes to ethical concerns, they will always revolve around staff and personnel issues. These are some of the most difficult to deal with. Our personal baggage influences our perspectives when dealing with these types of situations. During the process of earning my master's degree in educational leadership, we talked about this from a principal's point of view. But they don't prepare you for having these kinds of uncomfortable and difficult conversations.

Humility and confidence walk with you hand in hand when

CHAPTER 9: ETHICS

it comes to these types of issues. I thought I was ready to handle them. Looking back, I never took the time to think about how the ethical concerns would be seen by others or the individual themselves. I never thought about why they acted or did what they did. No thought about their feelings or their situation. I should have run through the scenarios in my mind before I called people in to have the tough talk. Think about asking these types of questions:

1. Tell me about the decision you made and how it affected this department.

2. What factors went into your decision-making process?

3. What do you believe I should do in this situation?

Having some simple brainstorming sessions will help you to be ready to confront the issue at hand. Consider what you would say if they outright lied to you. What if they get confrontational? Be prepared to answer them and be ready to face hard emotional choices. Stay strong and do so with humility and confidence in your ethical compass.

One example of this was during my review of department personnel files. I came across paperwork related to a request for an exemption from a state agency. The exemption was granted conditionally, with certain stipulations. My concern wasn't with the individual seeking the exemption; it was with the process and how it was handled. The chief officer involved had a personal connection to the individual that wasn't disclosed, and this raised some ethical concerns for me.

When I addressed the issue with the officer, the conversation didn't go as I had hoped. I pointed out that it would have been more appropriate for another member of the command staff to handle the request. It wasn't just about the exemption itself, but about maintaining transparency and integrity in the process.

This situation made me reflect on broader questions of leadership. Was this officer setting the right example for the team? Did their actions align with the ethical standards I expected?

Looking back, I see my approach could have been more balanced. I lacked the humility to recognize people may not always see things from my perspective, and I failed to approach the conversation with the understanding needed to create change. Instead, I came on too strong, which caused immediate defensiveness and created an enemy.

Humility in leadership means acknowledging we don't have all the answers, and others' perspectives, even when flawed, deserve to be considered. I should have approached the officer with a mindset of understanding, rather than accusation, seeking to uncover why they made the decision they did. Confidence, on the other hand, is knowing my ethical standards were correct and standing firm in them. However, true confidence also allows for calmness and patience in how those standards are communicated.

When faced with ethical challenges, tackle them head-on,

but with humility and confidence. Correcting the issue at hand while recognizing your approach is as important as the outcome.

Navigating Pressures and Ethical Challenges

As a leader, you'll face pressure from both the "top" and the "bottom." The top might be the board of directors, Police and Fire Commission, Village Board, City Council, Manager, or Mayor. They may believe they have political sway over you, as they ultimately approve or reject your budgets, personnel, and agenda. This political aspect of leadership is a reality you must navigate.

Pressure from the bottom comes from your staff. Their attitudes and beliefs drive the actual operations and team cohesion. If an influential staff member has done something wrong, you'll face pressure to go easy on them or look the other way. This pressure might manifest as tension or conversations that stop when you enter a room. Develop a thick skin to weather these kinds of storms.

To make ethical decisions, you need a defined moral compass. This is the core of who you are and what you believe is right or wrong. When I took over as Chief, I had pressures from both the top and bottom. As a leader, you're stuck in the middle, trying to make everyone happy while steering the ship in the right direction.

I got caught up in listening to too many opinions, including my own doubts. I mistakenly believed I had to shoulder everything myself, with all decisions starting and ending with me. The truth is, if your moral compass is guiding you, you'll be fine. Be transparent about your decision-making process, even with those outside your immediate team. Share how you approach choices, what factors matter, and invite others to contribute when it makes sense.

Poor ethical choices often happen when leaders feel backed into a corner. They may feel they have no choice but to go along with something questionable and hope no one finds out. But as they say, *how you do anything is how you do everything*. If everyone understands your expectations and decision-making process, you'll have fewer issues. When problems do arise, you can point to your previous communications.

As the one in charge, you set the tone for what's acceptable. Your role as an ethical leader is vital. Your words and actions will be scrutinized. You'll have supporters and detractors within your group. The character you portray and the ethics you possess will be visible to all.

Your role as an ethical leader will be filled with challenges. Don't look the other way when faced with ethical dilemmas. Address them promptly, but with tact and empathy. Use the right process and communication approach. Remember, your ethics and character are always on display. Stay true to your moral compass, be honest, and maintain rock-solid integrity. It's not just about making the right decisions - it's about how you make and communicate those decisions that define you as an ethical leader.

Lessons Learned:

1. Begin with transparency to establish trust from the start.

2. Addressing issues requires involving and educating your team, rather than assuming sole responsibility.

3. Balance humility and confidence in your approach, ensuring your decision-making process is transparent and well-communicated.

Chapter 10: Assistance

"NO ONE IS USELESS IN THIS WORLD WHO LIGHTENS THE BURDENS OF ANOTHER."

— CHARLES DICKENS

CHAPTER 10: ASSISTANCE

The Assistant EMS Chief burst into my office, frustration painted on her face and evident in her voice. "Chief, we need more staff! We've got too many open slots and not enough people to fill them. Everybody is exhausted, and we're struggling to cover calls. You need to do something now." I nodded, and said, "I know, I'm working on it." as she turned and left my office.

When I started as Fire Chief just a few months earlier, the department was understaffed by almost a third. It was a formidable challenge; one I had taken upon myself again to solve single-handedly. Day and night, I poured over applications and restructured schedules. I was burning the candle at both ends, and it was beginning to show.

One afternoon, as I stared blankly at yet another stack of papers and my computer screen, there was a knock at my door. One of our firefighters poked his head in. "Chief," he said hesitantly, "I couldn't help but notice you've been working non-stop on this staffing issue. I have some ideas that might help. Mind if I share them?"

As we talked, I realized he was qualified to assist and someone

I could trust to get the job done. We brainstormed ideas together, and before I knew it, he had set up a schedule and process for adding new staff and bringing others on board to help.

I was impressed by his skill and effort but also by the obvious reminder I didn't have to do it all myself. It was a humbling moment, one that would shape my approach to leadership in the months to come.

Sharing is Caring (And Sanity-Saving)

What I realized then, and what I'll tell you now, is this: don't be a hero. Trust me, no one's handing out medals for the leader who tried to do everything themselves. Ask for help when you need it. Don't try to do it all alone. Set your ego aside and discuss with your staff how they can help you and how you can help them. The quicker you involve your team, the quicker you realize you don't have to have all the answers. Create shared responsibility roles with your command staff. Asking for help and admitting you don't know it all will show you are humble and it will be respected.

Honesty and open conversations will lead to great discoveries. When you are open and honest about what you know and what you need to find out, it will enable those around you to show you what they may know and understand. Maybe they have the answer you are looking for. Maybe they know a subject matter expert or have a connection you haven't heard of yet. The point is, you never know unless you ask. So, ask.

CHAPTER 10: ASSISTANCE

It can be that simple.

When you try to change everything by yourself, you're just setting yourself up for failure, because you really think you can change everything yourself. You don't have the buy-in, you don't have the respect, and you're never going to achieve the real goal, which is to make the department better than you found it.

Involve those around you. They might not be the ones to answer the questions you have, but they can help share the load. There is always something that can be done. Share the work. Share the responsibility. Share the vision you have developed. When you include others, you are helping everyone become better. They might impress you with their untapped abilities and talent. They may be a diamond in the rough. You might even inspire further change and learning by doing so. They might even teach you a thing or two.

However, you might also find they will fail at their task. As a leader, you need to be OK with this. We all learn more from making mistakes and failing than from getting it correct right off the bat. Be patient and take a breath. And yes, when those mistakes happen, learn from them, correct them, and move on. It will be a process, it will take time. I know sometimes waiting for change to happen can be all-consuming; however, when you take a moment and allow the learning process to take place, everyone around you will be better for it, including yourself.

You Don't Have to Be the Know-It-All

As we become leaders, we think and assume we must have an answer every time. But this is not true. I used to tell my students I didn't know it all — or even a tiny fraction of it all — but we would figure out the answers together. You do not have to know everything about every topic as a leader. You need to know your weaknesses, embrace them, and not be afraid to share them but surround yourself with people who strengthen your weaknesses and challenge your understanding.

Trust the group of leaders who are around you. Talk to them and find out where they are strong and what their experiences are or what they have a passion for. If you learn they are weak in any area, then train them or provide resources where they can be developed. As a leader, you have to manage but also inspire. Some of this is done by being honest with yourself and with your team. So share your strengths and your weaknesses.

I went in with my ego held high and looked down on everyone in a command leadership role who had institutional knowledge because I thought I knew better, and I was hired for a reason. This is not the way to begin. Start by finding out who they are as people, what experiences they've had, and how they can help you. Sometimes you may find their experience far exceeds your own, they may even want to step back or help with something else. This is fine. Give them time and have the patience to understand a change in leadership can be a hard thing to process and accept. The important part to understand is you don't need to know it all, especially on day one.

The Art of Saying No

One of the biggest issues I've found is not being able to say NO. You don't have to agree with everything as if you're a bobblehead, politically or otherwise. Understand your limits and say no when you need to. No, you don't have the time for another project. No, you don't have the resources available. No, I can't think about it right now I've got too much on my plate. It is OK to say so. It is OK to recognize what you can and can't do.

That wasn't my attitude nor my belief when I started. I would go across the street nearly every other day to speak with the Village President and talk about the changes I was making and what my plans were. He would ask me to do more, and I said yes. The Clerk would see me and ask me to check on a budget item, and I said yes. The Public Works Director would find me in the hallway and ask me for a minute, and I would say yes. The answer I always had was yes. I wanted to do it all. I wanted to make everything right and do it all myself to show how great I was, how smart I was, and how awesome I was. Did I achieve those things? Absolutely not. I failed miserably. I agreed to do too much. Sure, I was able to make some superficial paper changes. I did improve some things in the short term. But in the end, I could have been more efficient and achieved more if I had said no more often.

Self-reflection is key. Reassess what's needed to achieve your vision and mission. Identify your available resources and what's missing. It's crucial to plan your time in the role—this higher level of organization will help you determine what's achievable and where other tasks might fit into your schedule.

If someone asks you to take on something that simply won't fit into your schedule, you have to be willing to say no. But I would add this important feature: explain to the person why. Let them know why you can't do it now, but maybe later, or maybe they can help you take something off of your plate in return. Have a discussion and communicate what your limitations are. Be honest and be open. They may not know how much you are trying to do; remember, we all have our perspectives, and we don't understand other people's lives until we walk in their shoes. Communicate your reasoning, and you will be amazed at what can happen.

Friends and Colleagues are Important

Being a leader can be a lonely place. Especially if you are at the top. Humans are social animals and we need others to help us and guide us. When you find yourself in a leadership position it is vitally important to connect with others in similar roles. I thought I could do it all myself and didn't need help. I was wrong. I reached out to a neighboring chief and we started to meet and talk about our similar situations and challenges. It became a highlight of my month when we would meet. Unfortunately, I found him too late in my journey. If I had him at the beginning I may have done things differently.

Finding a mentor can be a challenge. It takes faith and it takes courage to look for that person. We don't want to be seen as needing help, especially as Type-A personalities. But understand having trusted friends and colleagues, to ask for guidance or just be there to listen to our problems, can make all the difference.

The Power of Gratitude

It's crucial for leaders to acknowledge the efforts made by our team and those who help us. Expressing gratitude goes beyond politeness; it acknowledges their efforts and builds trust and respect. Authentic and real gratitude enhances morale and strengthens a feeling of a team, it will inspire people to exceed expectations. Nevertheless, sincerity is key. We can all tell when someone is genuine or not.

The feeling of gratitude operates in both directions. As much as you give it you've also got to be able to take it, but obviously do so with humility. Appreciation is an emotion that can directly affect peoples lives and attitudes toward us and our organizations.

From my personal experience, showing gratitude, whether through a hand-written note or a public recognition, has improved connections among my team members. By making gratitude a priority, we can create a positive environment where everyone feels appreciated and involved. So make it a priority to express your gratitude.

Lessons Learned:

1. Delegate responsibility to those who can help you.

2. Your time is limited and you need to say no when necessary.

3. Ask for help. Seek out a mentor.

Chapter 11: Communication

> "THE ART OF COMMUNICATION IS THE LANGUAGE OF LEADERSHIP."
>
> — JAMES HUMES

CHAPTER 11: COMMUNICATION

January 27, 2014

I turned my head and looked up at the clock on the wall of my office. 6:36 PM almost time to address the village board again. I let out an exhausted, sigh, as I pushed my chair away from my desk, got up, and walked out the door.

Let's back up this story just a bit. A month after I started the village board requested a report outlining my thoughts, goals, and a review of the department as a whole. This report became a guiding document for what I saw as needed change, and I used it as a springboard for all my subsequent actions and decisions.

Days turned into weeks as I pored through documents, procedures, protocols, and state statutes crafting what I thought was a comprehensive and forward-thinking plan for the department. But to my surprise, the report became a point of contention.

"Chief," one of the board members interrupted," are all these changes necessary? It seems... excessive."

You know you're in trouble when you hear, "necessary" as a

question.

"I mean, do we have to do all of these things?" said another board member.

"Well, yes." I expressed it abruptly. "We have to follow state laws and to do that we need to follow my plan."

When the board called my entire report into question, I took it as a personal attack. Angry and frustrated, I doubled down instead of reassessing my approach. I obtained a letter from the village lawyer based on the municipal insurance agency's position to follow state statutes by adopting National Fire Protection Association (NFPA) codes. I also received a letter from the state licensing agency stating the same, using these in my argument that the changes were not just suggestions but legal requirements.

The next week the board reluctantly agreed after I walked them through the rebuttal more slowly. However, I burned many bridges in the process. My poor choice to communicate my report and my presentation that day would ultimately be another factor in my downfall.

Listening and Connecting

Effective communication requires connection. This is why active listening is imperative for any leader. One of the most effective tools in communication is active listening yet it's proven more than 70% don't apply this method correctly. So, what is active listening? Well, it's simple. It occurs when you seriously listen, in other words not waiting you're turn to talk. You are focused on listening to the speaker, comprehending their words, their connotation, and body language. The only thing that matters is being present in the moment! Very few leaders practice this type of listening. Especially those who declare they are the best. Have you ever found yourself talking to someone who isn't listening to a word you're saying? How did you feel? Did you get angry? Now, imagine your staff feeling that way when communicating with you. As leaders, we must learn to shut up and be present. We need to be open to hearing different positions and opinions. Actively listen to those who are speaking to you.

Show a genuine desire for connection with your team. Find shared interests and demonstrate empathy to your staff. They are people too, remember! We all have our problems, concerns, and challenges in life. One is not more important than another, and we all face adversity. How we deal with it is what makes life worth living. The stories you tell and the stories your staff share will help you understand them as real people beyond just employees. Find those connections. Listen and learn.

One of the easiest ways to show connection is to maintain a calendar with birthdays, anniversaries, and special recognition of all your staff members. This will show them you care and will give credibility to your leadership style. Send out a birthday card or congratulations on achieving a new certification. But do it in person. Don't send out an email, go and talk to them. This simple act shows you care about them as individuals and carries far more weight than an impersonal standard form message.

The family atmosphere is highly sought after in the fire and emergency services, especially when you're working 24 hours a day with the same people. In the full-time realm, we end up spending a third of our adult lives with these colleagues. The last thing you want is to dread coming to work and look for ways to avoid it. Find the connections, find similar interests, find out who they are, and be open to sharing things about yourself too. Show empathy and show you do care about the person you are talking to.

Understanding and Perspective

As a leader, you will inevitably face strife, conflict, and tension. So, if or when you face this, what should you do? Should you go in guns blazing and rip those wounds open? Should you be brutally honest in your communication? I hope you have learned thus far that isn't the best and most productive strategy.

How I communicated with my staff was outright horrible. I failed miserably at bringing in the command staff to understand my way of thinking. I had assistant chiefs, captains, and lieutenants who all had many decades of experience and knew the village, its community, and the department far better than I. I chose to lump them all together and pushed them into the corner because they appeared to be fighting against me. You can only remedy this type of angst by sharing your

CHAPTER 11: COMMUNICATION

thoughts with the other side and finding mutual respect, understanding, and common ground.

This tense situation can worsen with the thought people may lose their identity, their position, or their place of importance. As I did with my command staff, I completely ostracized them. I cut them off from any and all engagement and leadership roles they had. I didn't communicate with them and even worse I didn't want to listen to what they had to say.

The problem was reinforced by my actions and my lack of honest and open communication. It causes mental stress on both parties and motivates those in opposition to do anything and everything in their power to keep things as they are used to. Change is hard, especially when it has been the status quo for so long people become complacent and at ease being in their comfort zone. Being confronted with a new way of thinking or, as I did, with a new leader, can have drastic implications.

To avoid this terrible issue, you need to be calm, and patient, and strive to create an environment of understanding. Bring people in and have frank discussions. Be open and honest with what you want to achieve and why. Be open in how you communicate your message and be willing to listen to their feedback. I've found many people just want to get it off their chest and say what they feel. Then it's over and they move on. As a leader, you need to sit back and let them speak. Let them yell and scream, but be patient in your response and be open to understanding a different point of view.

Mastering Hard Conversations

One of the hardest parts of leadership is navigating those difficult conversations. Whether it's delivering constructive feedback, addressing underperformance, or making tough decisions, these moments test our ability to communicate with both firmness and empathy. Looking back on my own experiences, I can say the tough conversations I've had were often the ones that pushed me to grow the most, as a leader and as a person.

During my college years, my academic advisor invited me to his office for a "*coming to Jesus meeting*". He didn't hold back any punches and bluntly told me my chosen path in electrical engineering wasn't right for me. He directed me toward teaching and coaching. It was a hard pill to swallow, but it made me reevaluate where I truly belonged. That conversation shaped my understanding of how necessary hard conversations are, even when they are uncomfortable.

In leadership, we often shy away from these moments, fearing conflict or hurt feelings. No one likes to be the bad guy. But avoidance leads to larger problems down the road. Hard conversations require us to be direct and honest while maintaining a sense of support and calm. Whether you're giving critical feedback or making tough calls about performance, the key is to approach these discussions with clarity and purpose. The "**sandwich method**" is a valuable tool, offering a positive attribute, then addressing the negative issue, and closing with another positive or offer of support.

Difficult conversations aren't about criticism or confrontation—they're about growth and they are about making the person better. As leaders, we must embrace these moments as opportunities to strengthen our teams and create a culture of open, honest communication. When done correctly those will become some of the best learning experiences. I've seen many people take the offer of support and grow. I have also seen people take the opportunity and flush it down the toilet. But as a leader, you have to understand not everyone will be your fan; take ownership of the situation and find out how you can be better as well as share how you are willing to work together to find the answers.

Non-Verbal Communication

What you say matters, but how you say it with your body also goes a long way. Body language is a huge part of our communication structures. Have you ever felt uncomfortable standing next to a person? Or watched someone give a speech you could feel their anxiety? Have you had a conversation with someone who was on their cell phone or had it on the table in front of them? These types of actions portray how we feel but also convey whether we are listening and paying attention to the speaker.

We pick up on these subtle clues. Sometimes they are consciously seen and other times they aren't. How we present our body language, how we express ourselves in our eyes, and where we look or don't look, will tell a lot about us. Think about the last time you felt someone wasn't listening to you. What were they doing? What did you see them do? When you communicate make sure your non-verbal actions are in line with what you are saying, avoid giving misguided signals. Facial expressions or how you look at a person, your smile, your arm gestures, and your tone of voice can convey sincerity, enthusiasm, and empathy. They all have clues to what you may think or feel. Emotions and attitudes often come across more through body language than words alone.

Non-verbal communication is vital because it shapes how messages are perceived and understood, adding depth to our interactions. Non-verbal aspects help what we say and provide additional context. A simple nod can reinforce agreement, while eye contact shows attentiveness. Consistent and positive non-verbal communication builds trust and credibility. It ensures our intentions are clear and strengthens our overall communication message. Put down your phone, uncross your arms, and focus on the person in front of you. Show interest in their thoughts and they will do the same.

Effective Communication Tips

Here are some of the most important tips I have found in communicating effectively.

> 1. Give your full attention to the speaker. Actively listen and focus on understanding their message before formulating your response. Show you're engaged through appropriate non-verbal cues and follow-up questions.

2. Easily express your ideas. Avoid jargon or details that might confuse your audience. Get to the point while ensuring your message is complete.

3. Try to understand the other person's perspective and feelings. This helps you create your message and respond appropriately. It also brings trust and openness to communication.

4. Think about your body language, facial expressions, and tone of voice with your words.

5. Ensure your message is understood by asking for feedback. Offer constructive feedback to others. This creates a communication loop.

Effective communication doesn't have to be complicated. Bring everyone in, sit down, talk, and discuss where we are and where we want to go together. It's as simple as that. The journey of leadership is challenging, and every interaction is an opportunity to grow and improve as a communicator.

Lessons Learned:

1. Build bridges rather than blow them up. Think about the message you are sending before you give it and how it will be heard.

2. Effective communication is not just about presenting your ideas; it's about listening and engaging with others and having empathy.

3. It's essential to communicate the reason behind decisions clearly and to be open to feedback. Ask questions and ensure the right non-verbal clues are given.

Chapter 12:
Engagement

"ENGAGEMENT IS THE EMOTIONAL COMMITMENT THE EMPLOYEE HAS TO THE ORGANIZATION AND ITS GOALS."

— KEVIN KRUSE

CHAPTER 12: ENGAGEMENT

The heavy door creaked open, as I slowly shuffled into my Freshman Chemistry 101 lecture hall, the soft buzz of nervous chatter filling my ears. Squeezing past knees and backpacks, I found a spot between two friends, our elbows bumping together as we settled into our chairs.

A hush fell over the student body as the Chemistry Professor strode onto the stage, his footsteps echoing in the sudden silence. He dropped a stack of transparencies onto the desk with a dull thud, the plastic sheets sliding across each other.

Click. Whir. Click. Whir.

One by one, the overhead projectors flickered to life, casting a hospital white glow across the lecture hall. The four screens are filled with a confusing array of formulas and equations, tiny symbols cramming into every available space.

The Professor's eyes darted between his watch and the wall clock. Without a word, he turned his back to us, facing the screens.

"Right, the molecular structure of..."

His monotone voice barely carried over the sudden rustle of paper and frantic scratching of pencils and pens. After an hour my hand cramped as I scribbled, desperately trying to keep pace.

The eerie silence in the hall was deafening. No one dared to whisper or even shift in their seat. The only sounds were desperate note-taking and the Professor's voice, with the occasional flip of the next plastic transparency sheet.

We've all endured mind-numbing classes with teachers who drone on endlessly. I've often wondered why these lectures aren't recorded and sold as sleep aids. As a leader, your ability to engage your staff is fundamental to your success. An engaged staff works harder, tries harder, and strives harder to accomplish the goals you set. They have a sense of commitment and involvement. Your success in engagement is directly linked to your communication skills and your ability to create the right environment.

In the chapters ahead, we'll explore engagement, inspiration, and motivation. While these concepts may seem closely related, each carries its own distinct meaning and impact. I believe they're important enough to explore them individually, as understanding their little nuances can make all the difference in being a successful leader.

The Role of Leadership in Engagement

Engagement isn't one-size-fits-all. It can take on many different forms depending on the individual and is best defined as the emotional commitment an employee has to the organization and its goals. The key word here is emotion. You engage with feeling. Engaging your staff is important because it will result in improved performance and increased retention.

As a leader, you obviously have to be the example to follow. The energy you bring sets the tone for the entire work environment. When you're all in—engaged and enthusiastic—it spreads. When you come in down and out everyone will feel it as well. But it's not just about showing up with a fake smile. It's about making sure your team knows why their work matters. People don't just engage with work tasks—they engage with meaning and feeling. When they see how their work ties into the bigger picture, their sense of purpose grows, and so does their commitment.

Strategies for Creating Engagement

1. Get to Know Your Staff

To create engagement, it's important to go back to the beginning and listen to your staff. Find out who they are and what makes them tick. Go through your personnel files. Learn about their lives, their families, their hobbies, and their interests. The more you know, the better prepared you will be to create a strategy on how to engage them.

Not only will this personalize your message, but it shows you have a genuine interest in them. Dale Carnegie's "How to

Win Friends and Influence People" teaches us remembering details about a person's life and interests can make them feel valued and respected, leading to higher engagement. This demonstrates you care for them and value them as whole people, not just workers.

2. Create Interactive Discussions

It doesn't have to be complicated. Start with something simple. Take trivia for example. I can't tell you how many lunches I sat in the firehouse kitchen watching old Jeopardy episodes trying to say the correct answer first with my crew. It was fun and we enjoyed the competition. But it also led to other questions and discussions.

Having an interactive discussion can be highly engaging. This strategy shows you are willing to discuss the issue or goal with everyone involved, but it also lends to the fact you are open and willing to hear different thoughts on the issue. It will build rapport with your staff and create an environment of psychological safety where employees feel secure in speaking up, sharing ideas, and even making mistakes.

Remember to use active listening and learn from the conversation. This will help to bring everyone onto the same page. Ask for opinions, encourage feedback, and start the questioning yourself. This approach shows your willingness to consider different perspectives and builds strong team relationships. Engaged employees often cite their relationships as a key reason they enjoy going to work.

3. Provide Meaningful Work and Recognition

For example, I always enjoyed hearing about successful EMS call outcomes. It was nice to know that the person we helped walked out of the hospital better than when we found them. This knowledge gives credit to the work and effort we put in on the job. It makes our purpose clear and it brings a sense of fulfillment to our work. That alone will go far with engaging your staff.

Recognition matters too, but it has to be genuine and sincere. Don't just praise the results—acknowledge the effort, the grind, and the personal touch they brought to the work. And it's not always about big saves or major accomplishments. Sometimes, it's as simple as remembering something personal about them or giving a nod to the small things they did to make a project succeed. A simple and honest thank you for cleaning up or helping to put items away when they didn't have to. Creating those personal connections will help to create trust and also will give you the ability to manage the team efforts more effectively. That connection is what sticks with people. It's the moments you notice them as individuals, not just their work.

4. Promote Growth and Autonomy

Engagement isn't just about professional growth. It's personal. People need to know they're not just filling a role—they're valued for who they are. You can offer training and opportunities for advancement, but if they don't feel seen or appreciated, it falls flat and no one will sign up for anything. The most engaged employees are the ones who feel they're growing and their contribution means something beyond just checking a box.

One of the best ways to show people they matter is to give them room to breathe. Trust them with autonomy. When you step back and let them figure out how to get things done, you're showing you believe in them and trust them. That trust builds confidence and, in turn, boosts engagement. People are more likely to invest in themselves when they know you're not watching their every move, waiting for them to mess up, and being a micromanager. They feel safer, and with safety comes creativity, ownership, engagement, and higher motivation.

5. Encourage Work-Life Balance

Because we're not robots we need balance. Recognize and respect their time outside the job. People can't engage fully if they're burned out or if they feel their personal life comes second to their work. Promoting a healthy work-life balance isn't just about being nice—it's about creating a positive environment where people can grow, both personally and professionally. Your team will be far more open to your engaging words when they see you recognize them as actual people.

Learning from Mistakes and Moving Forward

I learned these lessons the hard way. There was a time when I thought engagement meant telling people what to do and expecting them to blindly follow. I didn't create connections—I gave orders. And when things didn't go the way I wanted, I doubled down instead of stepping back and reassessing. The approach didn't just fail—it backfired in my face. Engagement requires investment upfront. It's not about the big speeches or bold directives. It's about doing the work, connecting with your people, and understanding what drives them before you even get to the "big moments."

At the end of the day, an engaged person will always remember how you made them feel and how important you made them feel. That's what matters. That's what drives real engagement.

Engagement doesn't have to be overly complicated. Regularly assess engagement levels through surveys, one-on-one discussions, and team meetings. Write down what worked and what didn't. Use this data to continually improve your engagement strategies. By doing so, you'll create a positive environment where employees are truly committed to their work and the organization's success.

My Chemistry Professor and I didn't think about how serious engagement can affect the people around you. It can make or break your attitude of not only your team but all of those who interact with them as well. Engagement takes time and skill to be used effectively. Make sure you find the time.

Lessons Learned:

1. Invest time in building personal connections with your team from the start.

2. Leave them alone don't micromanage! Give them the freedom to fail and succeed.

3. Recognize their efforts and share their success stories to show how their work matters.

Chapter 13:
Inspiration

"IF YOUR ACTIONS INSPIRE OTHERS TO DREAM MORE, LEARN MORE, DO MORE, AND BECOME MORE, YOU ARE A LEADER."

— JOHN QUINCY ADAMS

CHAPTER 13: INSPIRATION

September 30, 2013

The fire station's conference room buzzed with low chatter as I stepped inside. Familiar faces mixed with new ones, all turning to look at me. My new white shirt felt stiff and the gold badge felt heavy as I walked into the room. I cleared my throat.

"Good evening, everyone," I said, my voice echoing slightly in the now-silent room.

I plugged in my laptop and flipped the button on the projector as it hummed to life. The title slide of my PowerPoint presentation glowed on the screen behind me.

"As your new Fire Chief, I'm excited to share my vision for the future of this department," I began, launching into the speech I'd rehearsed countless times in my drive to the station.

But after ten minutes, I noticed a few sets of eyes starting to look at the clock, then hidden yawns, and a Lieutenant's blurry gaze was fixed on a point somewhere just behind my left shoulder.

I ignored it all and pressed on, flipping through slides crammed with bullet points and charts. The room felt increasingly stuffy and warm. "Was the AC even working?" I thought to myself.

A little more than halfway through my grand plan for restructuring, I caught sight of a young firefighter. He was fighting a losing battle to keep his eyes open. Trying so hard not to fall asleep.

My words started to trail off. I looked down at my notes, then back at the sea of blank zombielike faces. The awkward silence in the room was palpable.

"So, uh... any questions?" I asked apprehensively, knowing full well there wouldn't be any.

A few polite coughs. Someone shifted in their chair.

"Right," I said, snapping my laptop shut. "We'll... pick this up another time. Thank you."

As everyone filed out, relief painted on their faces, I walked back to my small office and slumped into a chair. So much for my big debut as Chief. I lost them before I'd even begun.

That day taught me a harsh lesson about the difference between speaking and truly inspiring and I knew better.

The Power of Storytelling

As a teacher, I always start with a story. And if you haven't caught on yet as an author as well. Stories inspire me. I love to read and listen to them. The tales of great heroism and overcoming challenges are ones I try to learn from. How we get inspired differs from person to person, which is why implementing multiple approaches is crucial.

Storytelling is a powerful tool for both inspiration and engagement. It's a terrific way to grab attention and make your message memorable. If you want your group to strive to become more proficient with turnout times, tell a tale about how one department achieved it. What did they do? How did they reach their goal? Make the story interesting and entertaining. Memorable stories will become inspirational because of the lessons they can teach.

Once you've researched your staff or audience, find a story that contributes to the inspirational message you want to deliver. The story can be one of your own, or it can come from any other source - just make sure you credit where it's from. Storytelling provides context and illustration, allowing listeners to imagine what you're saying. This creates lasting memories, evokes emotions, and imparts a compelling, lasting value. As a leader, a well-chosen story can set the right mood and bring your staff together around a common theme or vision.

When you tell a story, you're not just conveying information; you're painting a picture of possibilities. You want to show your team how they can achieve the goal and how YOU will help them do it. Start with a story, and you'll find your audience more receptive to the challenges and opportunities ahead.

Inspiring Drive and Hope

"...We choose to go to the Moon in this decade and do the other things, not because they are easy, but because they are hard; because that goal will serve to organize and measure the best of our energies and skills..."

-President John F. Kennedy September 12, 1962.

Why is the pen mightier than the sword? Because there is great power in words. When you are inspired to achieve, nothing can stop your drive to do so. As a leader, it's your job to bring inspiration to your team. President Kennedy made this speech fully understanding how impossible the task would be. The National Air and Space Administration (NASA) could barely get a man into orbit and back safely, let alone reach the moon, land, and return home. An inspirational message can motivate others to dream of possibilities. Those dreams can become goals, and those goals can become reality with the right inspiration.

Inspiration is also about feeling and emotion too. The mental stimulation you feel, or the need to act, or be a part of something special. Like President Kennedy's vision of space exploration. If you would go back to the 1960s and ask anyone who worked at NASA what their job was they would all tell

CHAPTER 13: INSPIRATION

you they were working to put a man on the moon. Everyone would say this from the top engineers to the secretaries and janitors. Everyone was inspired to do their part to achieve the goal. They understood the story they were a part of. The inspiration to get there is the start, but drive and motivation will fuel you to achieve the goal. You cannot do one without the other. Words will inspire those aspects you need to rely on as a leader.

When I became Fire Chief, I assumed my staff would automatically listen and understand my message. I didn't consider how I delivered the message or the spirit behind it. I didn't even give one thought about whether I was saying anything inspirational or not. I assumed my position gave me authority and others would blindly follow.

The fact is we're all unique individuals, shaped by diverse backgrounds and experiences. This diversity extends to our drive and what we use for inspiration. What makes this mistake harder to understand is that, as a former teacher and athletic coach, I know how inspiration can drive a person. Some people are driven by the need for money, title, or prestige. Others are driven by family and friendship. What matters most goes back to what I've said before; to take the time to understand your team and what makes them unique. Focus on their needs and how you can inspire them through your messaging. Understand what inspires them to act.

Hope also has a major role here. Your inspirational message and your power of leadership is one that deals with your ability to drive hope. Hope will give your team something to look forward to, to see how things could be better, more productive, and more efficient. The hope for a better tomorrow. This type of feeling, with creative messaging, will lead to the inspiration you seek.

Once you have molded and crafted the message and have given the people something to aspire to and hope for, then the inspiration to see it through will be amazing. You will be shocked at what actions will occur naturally. The process will start, and the change you seek will be within your team's grasp. All because of the hope you have inspired.

Leading with Heart

You've got to show the love! Yes, you read that right. One of the biggest mistakes I made was neglecting to show my team that I valued them by actually showing my care and love for them. Now, I don't mean getting all huggy and holding hands while singing kumbaya, but as a leader, it's important to show your emotions and let your team know you genuinely care. It's okay, and it's necessary, to show that you love your team in a way that creates respect and connection. That is a huge part of inspiration for anyone.

Showing care and love for your people goes beyond saying "thank you." It's about what you *do*. Staying late to help finish a task after a long day, stepping out of your office to help other finish a project, or even taking the time to clean the trucks or bathrooms alongside them—it's these actions that resonate and show you care. Little things like offering to watch the oven during lunch may seem small, but they go a long way in building trust. Studies show that when employees feel seen and supported, they are more engaged, motivated, and inspired. People respond when they know their leader isn't just barking orders from on high but is in the trenches with them. It's this kind of care that inspires people to go the extra mile—not because they have to, but because they want to. Show your love.

Communicate Inspiration the Right Way

This will only happen if you do it the right way. You simply cannot tell people what to think and how to act. Great leaders show and illustrate the actions they want to see emulated. They are the model for the crews to witness. *Talk is cheap.* Be an example of the inspiration you want to see. Lead. If you sit behind a desk and send out emails, they will go nowhere and inspire nothing. You can write the best book in the world, but if no one reads it, what change will you inspire from the words you have written?

Learning how to communicate your message of inspiration is crucial to your success. Whether you are telling a story or showing empathy it needs to be done sincerely and from a place of actual integrity. Your staff and team will feel your message as we talked about earlier. I made the mistake of assuming everyone wanted the same things I did as a leader. I was wrong. Take the time to create a hopeful and inspiring thought that will drive your team to success.

Lessons Learned:

1. Storytelling can be an exceptional way to deliver a message and create inspiration.

2. Learn about your team and what they value. Then craft your inspirational message to them.

3. Hope can drive us to accomplish great things in life. Inspire hope by being the example to follow.

Chapter 14: Motivation

"YOU ARE NEVER TOO OLD TO SET ANOTHER GOAL OR TO DREAM A NEW DREAM."

— C.S. LEWIS

CHAPTER 14: MOTIVATION

In 1970, UCLA was in the NCAA Men's Championship Basketball Game against Jacksonville University. At halftime, UCLA was ahead by 5 points. The players entered their locker room tired and worried.

To the teams surprise, Head Coach John Wooden calmly walked in and said, "Men, let's go over the fundamentals." He then gathered the team around him and demonstrated how to put on their socks and shoes properly, just as he had done on day one at the beginning of the season.

This wasn't a fiery oh-ra-ra motivational speech. Instead, it reminded them of the basics, the little things, and the foundation of their success that season. But it also served to calm the players' nerves by focusing their attention on a simple, familiar task, something they could do in their sleep.

One of the players, Sidney Wicks, later recalled, "We're all sitting there thinking, 'What's he doing?' But what he was doing was getting our minds off the pressure of the game."

Coach Wooden's unconventional approach worked. The players left the locker room relaxed and refocused and with new energy in their shoes. They went on to win the game and secure yet another NCAA championship.

John Wooden is known for his unique style of motivation. Rather than relying on emotional speeches or harsh criticism, he motivated his team by reinforcing the fundamentals and helping them stay calm under pressure. He understood sometimes, the best motivation comes from reminding people of what they already know and helping them focus on the process rather than the outcome.

Wooden's approach worked not just in this game, but throughout his career. His teams won an unbelievable 10 NCAA championships in 12 years, and many of his players have cited his calm, focused approach as a key factor in their success.

Effective motivation doesn't always involve grand actions or inspirational speeches. Sometimes, it's about helping people return to their foundations, stay calm under pressure, and focus on what they can control.

As leaders, we often focus on strategy, decision-making, and achieving targets. However, two critical elements of effective leadership are frequently overlooked: showing appreciation and maintaining motivation. These factors can significantly impact your success as a leader and the overall performance of your team.

CHAPTER 14: MOTIVATION

Understanding Motivation

Motivation is the driving force that compels us to take action. It stems from our deepest desires, ambitions, and the vision we hold for our future. Without motivation, it's difficult to gather energy to chase our goals. But motivation alone isn't enough – it needs the partnership of discipline to see us through to the finish line.

There are two primary personal motivators:

1. **Intrinsic Motivation:** This comes from within. It's the internal drive to achieve something for personal satisfaction or fulfillment. Pursuing work, you do because it brings you joy and a sense of accomplishment. That's intrinsic motivation at work.

2. **Extrinsic Motivation:** This is fueled by external factors such as money, rewards, recognition, or avoiding negative consequences. Working hard to land a promotion or bonus, or completing a project on time to avoid your boss's criticism are examples of extrinsic motivation.

Both types of motivation can be powerful drivers. The key is to identify which one resonates more with you and your team. If you're intrinsically motivated, tap into that inner fire and interest to fuel your journey. If external rewards or recognition are your thing, leverage them as your driving force. But don't deny them, use them to the best of your abilities to achieve.

The Power of Appreciation

Early in my career as a fire chief, I made a critical mistake many new leaders fall victim to – I failed to show appreciation for my team. From the lack of a proper swear-in ceremony to my dictatorial approach, I missed numerous opportunities to acknowledge the hard work and dedication of my staff. It's a regret that stays with me to this day.

Your staff is the backbone of your organization. You can have the most advanced multi-million dollar equipment and cutting-edge technology, but without capable hands to operate them, they're worthless. When you step into a leadership role, you're entrusted with the responsibility of not just managing resources but nurturing and developing your team.

Coach Wooden understood this very well. In his "Pyramid of Success", he placed team spirit near the top, emphasizing the importance of unity and consideration for others. He believed genuine appreciation for each team member's contribution was crucial to encouraging this spirit.

As we talked about with engagement showing appreciation doesn't require anything special. Often, it's the small, and honest acts of recognition that have the most impact:

- A sincere "thank you" delivered with eye contact, a handshake, or a high-five.

- Public praise for a job well done.

- Bringing in treats such as ice cream or doughnuts or making lunch for the team.

These simple actions can go a long way in building morale, creating loyalty, and building a positive work environment. They will show your crew their efforts are seen and valued, which in turn motivates them to continue performing at their best. Simply show them the appreciation they deserve.

The Dual Nature of Motivation

There's an old Cherokee parable tale of two wolves who battle within each of us. One wolf embodies negative traits such as anger, envy, and sorrow, while the other represents positive qualities such as joy, compassion, and empathy. The wolf we chose to feed is the one who wins our internal struggle.

This parable perfectly illustrates the importance of nurturing the right motivations, both within ourselves and within our teams. As a leader, it's important to take time and reflect on your motivations. As we discussed regarding ambition, what drives you to lead? Are you seeking this position for the right reasons? How do you maintain your motivation during challenging times? Your internal motivation is the fuel which powers your leadership journey. It's what gives you the discipline to push through obstacles and the strength to get back up when you fall.

This discipline relates directly to the intrinsic factor. How we make others feel about themselves and about their work. If your crew went above and beyond call it out as an example to follow. If a community group donated something, then give them a shoutout on social media. You have the power to put a spotlight on these positive highlights.

As Chief, I fed the wrong wolf far too often and I also didn't feed the right wolf in others. When you feed the wrong wolf, you will destroy any motivation that could exist. Take a serious look at what you are doing as a leader and whether you are making things better or worse.

The Role of Discipline

Discipline is the practice of training yourself to follow a specific code of behavior or way of thinking. It involves self-control, firm commitment, and relentless consistency. While motivation gets you started, discipline is the engine that keeps you going, especially when the initial burst of motivation starts to fade.

Remember the New Year's resolution you abandoned after a few weeks? Or the promise you made to yourself only to forget about it later? That's where discipline comes in. It's the force that compels you to stick to your plans and routines, even when motivation starts to dwindle.

Motivation and discipline aren't rivals; they complement each other beautifully. Motivation gives you a sense of purpose and direction, while discipline provides the structure to push yourself toward that purpose. How you accomplish this as the leader will take time and knowledge of your staff. Discipline

CHAPTER 14: MOTIVATION

isn't just yelling or punishing. It is set by ourselves to **WANT** to achieve the goal we have. As leaders, we need to ensure our staff are equipped to set the right discipline factor and combine it with the right motivation.

Achieving a balance between motivation and discipline can be challenging, but it's the cornerstone of long-term success. Here are some practical tips to help find the equilibrium:

1. **Set Goals:** Define what you want to accomplish, ensure you can track your progress, set realistic and attainable goals, choose goals that align with your values, and establish deadlines to create a sense of urgency.

2. **Develop a Routine:** Creating a daily or weekly routine fosters discipline. A consistent schedule minimizes the need for constant decision-making and keeps you on track. Experiment to find a routine that complements your lifestyle and goals.

3. **Embrace Positive Reinforcement:** Reward yourself and your team for staying disciplined. Positive reinforcement strengthens motivation and reinforces the habit of discipline. Treat yourself to a small indulgence or activity you enjoy after reaching a milestone or sticking to your routine for a set period.

4. **Stay Accountable:** Share your goals with a trusted friend or family member, or join a group focused on similar objectives. Accountability partners provide

support, encouragement, and a gentle nudge when you need it most.

5. **Reflect and Adjust:** Regularly review your progress. Reflect on what's working and what's not. Don't be afraid to pivot or modify your approach if something isn't working. Self-reflection is key to optimizing your strategy.

Walking the Talk

When I became chief, I showed my appreciation far too rarely. I didn't take the time to express my gratitude to my crew for the great work they did. I missed opportunities to hand out small tokens of appreciation such as a simple thank you, especially significant as I was their first full-time chief.

These may seem like minor oversights, but in leadership, it's often the small things that make the biggest difference. They're the building blocks of trust, respect, and loyalty – essential components of any high-performing championship group.

Make a conscious effort to incorporate appreciation into your daily leadership. Set a goal to recognize at least one member each day. Keep a supply of cards in your desk, ready to jot down a quick message of appreciation when you notice exceptional effort. But the important part here is to recognize it must be done sincerely and honestly. We can all tell when someone does something because they **have** to. Show appreciation because you **want** to. Praise in public and praise the exceptional work being done.

As for motivation, start by examining your own. Are you feeding the right wolf? Are your actions aligned with your values and the greater good of your team and organization? Then, take time to understand what drives each of your team members. Use this knowledge to create a motivational strategy that resonates with everyone while also addressing their individual motivational factors.

Remember, as a leader, your attitude and energy are contagious. By maintaining a positive outlook and consistently showing appreciation, you set the tone for your entire organization. You have the power to create an environment where people feel valued, motivated, and inspired to give their best every day.

Just as Coach Wooden's focus on the fundamentals led to unprecedented success, your attention to the basic human needs for appreciation and motivation can lead to extraordinary achievements. Remember, it's not just about tying shoelaces or straightening socks - it's about showing every detail matters, their efforts are valued, and together, you can accomplish greatness with the right motivation.

Lessons Learned:

1. Motivation doesn't have to be big speeches but a reminder to stay calm and take care of the little things first.

2. Show your team you appreciate them by speaking to them honestly and sincerely.

3. Feed the right wolf, don't give in to the negative but stay positive and keep your head up showing the way.

Chapter 15: Teams

"COMING TOGETHER IS A BEGINNING. KEEPING TOGETHER IS PROGRESS. WORKING TOGETHER IS SUCCESS."

— HENRY FORD

CHAPTER 15: TEAMS

The late August heat was suffocating. My body was exhausted, and every movement felt like a chore. I bent down to touch the end line, my muscles screaming to stop with every step.

Coach Johnson, a man built as solid as a brick wall with a voice to match, shouted, "Again!" His weathered face showed no sympathy as our team staggered back to the opposite sideline.

"Don't be last, Hill!" Johnson barked. "The beatings will continue until morale improves!" His attempt at humor fell flat in the oppressive heat.

As I ran, my legs felt as heavy as concrete blocks, and I wondered how much longer we could keep this up. But then I remembered why we were here - to be the best, to be unbeatable. The pain was temporary, but the glory would last forever. Next to me my friend Tim was breathing hard and started to cough. The echoes of retching started as some were throwing up down the line.

Years later, long after my cleats were lost in a closet, I realized those hellish practices were about more than just physical conditioning. They were making us into a cohesive unit, teaching us teamwork.

Throughout my life, I've been part of many teams. Football, track, broomball, activity groups, teaching - you name it, I've been there. Each experience reinforced one crucial lesson: the power of a strong team and unity. It's a topic countless successful coaches have written about, and their insights offer valuable knowledge for anyone in a leadership position.

The Cornerstone of a Team

I've been a part of some great teams and some not-so-terrific teams, including the one I led. But what I have found is great coaches, the ones who consistently lead their teams to victory, share some common methods. They create environments built on three key pillars: competition, safety, and spirit. In these environments, members feel they can work together towards a shared common goal. They strive to be their best, not for the coach's sake, but for the team as a whole - for each other. It's more than just a group; it's a family.

This team aspect is communal, forged through shared experiences and, often, shared pain. Through these trials and tribulations, we build faith and trust in one another. We know, without a doubt, the person next to us is willing to fight and die. In the emergency services, this bond is key. We rely on each other no matter the situation or how dangerous it might be. The team aspect is vital and pivotal to engage and create trust in each other. The department is a family, as dysfunctional as it might be sometimes, it's the family spirit and attitude that keeps us coming back.

Great teams also have a shared sense of responsibility. Players are asked to be leaders for their groups, with more experienced veterans guiding younger teammates. The veterans are looked up to by the greenhorns, the younger and less experienced, to show them the way, to set the example, and to be their mentors. Strong teams rely on this aspect and count on the players to police themselves. They openly encourage members to get better and use peer support and pressure to accomplish this, hopefully in a positive manner.

The Fun Factor

Highly functioning teams also have fun. They focus on winning and the positive excitement which comes with trying hard to achieve victory. This doesn't have to be done in a game but can be applied to every little task. Small victories often lead to great accomplishments down the road. When you make work fun, you create a path to success worth striving for. Camaraderie, laughter, joking around, and bonding in this fashion all lead to better team chemistry and a stronger realization of how connected they are to each other. The bond becomes set in stone.

So, how can we accomplish this? Well, it's simpler than you think. Make training fun by incorporating friendly competition between teams. Engine company versus Truck company. Sales versus Marketing. The reward could be a traveling trophy or something as simple as leaving for lunch earlier than the rest. Create ways to make work fun by having a "Dad Joke" of the day or finding a funny meme and sharing it with the group. There are many ways you can do this and make it have value for the team bonding and atmosphere you would want to work in yourself.

Building a strong team is something every leader needs to prioritize. As chief, I failed to do this at every step I took. And again, I knew better as a former coach. Athletics illustrate this point. How many poorly performing teams, who don't win a game, replace the head coach and wind up becoming champions the following year with the same players. What was the catalyst for this drastic improvement? How'd this miracle happen? Leadership. The head coach and his support staff made all the difference. If you have a great coach who knows what to do and how to achieve greatness, then your team will go far. They create a positive working environment the team will use to win, have fun, and become champions.

The Power of Tradition

When I became chief I neglected to find out if the department had any traditions. Were there anniversaries, or other dates that were celebrated or important? Was there a song or type of music that was special? Find out what the department traditions are and celebrate them, embrace them no matter how ridiculous they may seem to you. Find a way to positively use them.

Championship teams always have great traditions. Many college football teams incorporate "the walk." This tradition was first started by Coach Bear Bryant at the University of Alabama, where his team would meet at Denny Chimes, a landmark on campus, and walk together to the football stadium as a team, a family. They would encounter fans and supporters on the way. It became a tradition that, decades later, has spread to many other campuses.

Another powerful example is the New Zealand Rugby Team's Haka dance performed before the competition. This long-standing tradition shows the unity and strength of the team and their connection to the Māori native people of the islands they represent. The dance is done in unison and shows the team working together and firing themselves up as well as intimidating their opponents.

Traditions built upon unity and togetherness are often overlooked by leaders. But they are pivotal to the success you will have in creating any team mentality and environment. These traditions can be old or new. Investigate and find out if there are any. If there aren't, then create some new ones with the help of your staff. Find out what people like to do and how they enjoy spending their time. Find a common connection to establish a tradition.

The Impact of Champions

Building a strong team isn't just about assembling talented individuals. It's about creating an environment where those individuals can thrive together, where they're motivated not just by personal success but by the success of the group. This foundation of team culture is rooted in the same principles Coach Lou Holtz, Urban Meyer, and Nick Saban emphasized in their championship football programs.

In *Winning Every Day*, Coach Lou Holtz stresses the importance of setting high standards, a relentless pursuit of excellence, and a passion for perfection. These principles are the cornerstone of any great team, whether in sports or emergency services. This means not just striving for personal excellence but holding each other accountable and committing to continuous improvement. Ask yourself:

1. Am I committed to pursuing perfection?

2. Do I accept bad behavior, or do I look the other way?

3. Can I do more to set the example?

Your team's foundation must be rooted in these core principles. A lack of structure will lead to a collapse when tested by the challenges of our work.

Coach Urban Meyer's, Above-the-line mindset reinforces this idea. He divides behavior into two categories—actions are either above or below the line of acceptance. Encouraging above-the-line behavior means celebrating punctuality, hard work, and leadership, while swiftly addressing negative actions. These behaviors form the walls of a champion team—walls to protect the culture from crumbling under stress.

CHAPTER 15: TEAMS

Once you've established a strong foundation and built the walls of positive behaviors, you must continuously evaluate and improve. As Coach Nick Saban describes in *How Good Do You Want to Be?*, improvement requires constant reflection. Did your team get better today? How are you improving your weaknesses? This process of reevaluation is like putting a roof on your building—it seals in success and ensures your team can withstand future storms.

Remember, a strong team can achieve far more than even the most talented individual. As a fire chief, I learned this lesson the hard way. Prioritize team building from day one, and watch as your group transforms from a collection of individuals into a cohesive, unstoppable group. After all, in the face of life's challenges - whether on the sports field, in the boardroom, or battling a five-alarm fire - there's nothing more powerful than a team that stands united, ready to face whatever comes their way together.

Lessons Learned:

1. Successful teams are built on three key pillars: competition, safety, and spirit.

2. Prioritize building strong teams that have fun and are willing and able to achieve their goals.

3. Don't overlook traditions, use them, build on them, and create new ones to encompass every member of your team.

Chapter 16: Goals

"IF YOU WANT TO BE HAPPY, SET A GOAL THAT COMMANDS YOUR THOUGHTS, LIBERATES YOUR ENERGY, AND INSPIRES YOUR HOPES."

— ANDREW CARNEGIE

CHAPTER 16: GOALS

If it isn't apparent to you by now, I didn't have real leadership goals. Sure, I had goals—personal ones, ones which fed my ego and made me look good, or so I thought. I had a vision, but it wasn't grounded in the reality of what the team needed. These goals were mine alone. There was no buy-in, no sense of shared purpose, and no one felt compelled to achieve them.

That's the mistake leaders make; confusing personal ambition with organizational goals. And I was no different. It wasn't until things started slipping through the cracks—projects stagnating and motivation dwindling—I realized I had failed to inspire by setting shared goals. The goals weren't about them. They weren't about the department's future or the collective good. They were all about me. And that's not how leadership works.

Take Steve Jobs, for example. When he returned to Apple as CEO in 1997, he didn't just set personal goals. He created goals the entire company could rally around. Apple was on the brink of bankruptcy, and Jobs had to reignite the fire that once made Apple stand out. He set bold, clear goals that were more than just his own; they became the company's goals. It wasn't just about bringing back innovation—it was about making the team believe they could achieve something groundbreaking together. Within just a few years Apple introduced a series of revolutionary products, including the iMac, iBook, iPod, iTunes Store, iPod mini, MacBook, iPhone, and Apple TV.

That's the difference between real leadership and self-serving ambition: the ability to set goals which inspire and drive your team toward a common purpose.

The Importance of Goal Setting

Goal setting is something we all need to work on, but it is imperative to have as a leader. Goal setting directly contributes to your vision and mission. Daily, weekly, monthly, quarterly, yearly, and long-term goals should all be established. Discuss these goals with your staff and crew. Involve as many as possible to gather information, thoughts, beliefs, and opinions. Once you have as much information as possible then sit down and evaluate what you have and what you need. Plan with your staff and bring in all those who will be responsible for the achievement of the goals you decide to set. As Benjamin Franklin said, "*If you fail to plan, you are planning to fail.*"

Let's break this down a bit. When I talk about goal setting, I'm not just talking about having a vague idea of where you want to be in five years. I'm talking about a comprehensive approach to goal setting that covers everything from what you want to achieve today to where you want your organization to be in a decade.

A simple tool for this are SMART Goals which stand for: specific, measurable, achievable, relevant, and time-bound. This isn't just another acronym but a practical way to set goals that mean something. Here's how you can use them:

Specific- Don't be vague with the goal. For instance, saying "get in shape" is not good enough. Be specific such as I will run a 5k.

Measurable- Saying you want to "do more" or "be better" isn't measurable. Put a number down like I will run the 5k in under 40 minutes.

Achievable- This is a bit more tricky. Don't set yourself up for failure but be realistic. If you've never run a 5k before then saying run a 5k every day is out of reach. Instead say you want to run 1 mile a day for the next 2 weeks.

Relevant- This means the goal matters to you and where you want to be. If you want to get into better shape by losing 30 pounds then selecting a goal to finger paint isn't relevant to the mission. Mastering your meals is far more in line.

Time- This is the limit, the deadline. A goal without a deadline is just a wish. Put a date on it. I will run the 5k within the next 6 weeks in under 40 minutes.

Goals are very important because they give you something to aim for. But they have to be something you can achieve. It's not magic to be successful but it does take planning. Set goals your team helps to create and set goals designed to benefit the organization as a whole and not you as the leader.

Involving Your Team

Here we go involving other people again! Yes, the key here is these goals can't just come from you as the leader. You've got to involve your team in the process. When I was chief, one of my biggest mistakes was setting goals in isolation. I thought I knew what was best, I didn't take the time to understand what my team thought we needed to focus on. I assumed whatever they were doing was wrong and I threw everything out. Involve your team to find out what kinds of goals they have and see how they can be improved. Their department goals might be great and don't need to be changed. But you will never know unless you ask them.

For example, in the fire service, a team's daily goal might be to complete all equipment checks without any issues found. A weekly goal could be to run a certain number of training drills. A monthly goal might involve completing a specific number of fire safety inspections in the community. Quarterly, you might aim to reduce response times by a certain percentage. Yearly, you could set a goal to implement a new community outreach program. And the long term, you might have a goal to build a new fire station or implement a major new firefighting technology.

Your team can help you and can lift the load. Involve them,

ask them, and see how they can assist you in the process.

Organizing for Success

Organization and goal setting are linked together. The organization and structure all have a role to play in your ability to set clear goals.

First, your organization needs a solid structure. It's not just about having a fancy flowchart. It's about knowing who does what, when, and why. Who's calling the shots? Where do we go when problems arise? How do we get things done without tripping over each other? These aren't just random questions they're the backbone of your department's organization.

Your organizational structure should be a roadmap to your goals. They're not separate entities. For instance, let's say you want to improve community relations. Terrific, but it's just talk without an organizational structure to back it up. Who's leading the mission on this? How does it fit into everyone else's responsibilities? How are we measuring success? Your organizational structure should answer those questions.

Now, I screwed this up when I became chief. I walked in with a new organization chart before I even talked to anyone. I set goals that were "mine," created an organization that was "mine," and wondered why nobody was as excited as I was. I was trying to jam my square peg into the round hole of reality.

As the leader, you've got to think long-term as well. A

five-year plan isn't just a pipe dream - it's a necessity. Remember the Cathedral concept? Those long-term goals need to be broken down into bite-sized chunks that fit into your organizational structure. Maybe you're aiming to build a new station in ten years. Great. But how does that translate to what each team member does day-to-day? How will that big goal help your other small goals your team set? Your organizational structure should make it clear to help bring about the long-term needs.

Remember, your goals and your organization aren't separate entities. They're two parts of the machine, working together to drive your department forward. Get them in sync, and you'll be amazed at what you can achieve.

Maintaining Momentum

When I finally learned my lesson and started involving my team in goal setting, we came up with a plan everyone was excited about. It included things like designing a new fire station, upgrading our fleet with more capable vehicles, and establishing a joint training program with neighboring departments.

We broke these big goals down into smaller, achievable milestones. And here's the key: we celebrated every win, no matter how small. When we completed our first joint training exercise, we had a barbecue with the other department. These celebrations weren't just about patting ourselves on the back. They were about reinforcing our shared goals as a team and keeping everyone motivated and inspired.

It all goes back to communication. Sure, it may seem difficult at first when you arrive at a new place or in a new role. That is to be expected and understand you are not alone in this feeling. Everyone is anxious and uncertain at first. But even if some massive needs and changes have to be made just take them one at a time. Find the most critical first and then move toward other issues you can deal with later. But involve your staff. Allow them to help you. Show you want their opinions and value their thoughts. Empower the leaders within your group. All of this can lead to success in your goal-setting. Take time and have patience.

Lessons Learned:

1. Involve your team in the goal-setting process from the beginning.

2. Break down long-term goals into smaller, achievable milestones to maintain momentum and celebrate progress.

3. Align your organizational structure with your goals to ensure clarity and efficiency in achieving them.

Chapter 17:
Challenges

"OBSTACLES DON'T HAVE TO STOP YOU. IF YOU RUN INTO A WALL, DON'T TURN AROUND AND GIVE UP. FIGURE OUT HOW TO CLIMB IT, GO THROUGH IT, OR WORK AROUND IT."

— MICHAEL JORDAN

CHAPTER 17: CHALLENGES

August 12, 2013

The gleaming red ladder truck appeared before me as I followed the day crew on my first tour of the fire station. Pride radiated from their faces as they gestured toward the massive vehicle.

"And here's where we keep some of our most important equipment," one firefighter announced, rolling up the side compartment door.

My eyes widened as I looked inside. Two enormous spools of extension cord dominated the space, each holding what must have been 500 feet of heavy-duty extension cord.

"What are those for?" I asked, trying to keep my voice neutral and inquisitive.

The firefighter reached past the spools and pulled out two objects that made my jaw drop. In his hands were a pair of electric chainsaws, their black and orange casings faded and scratched. The model stamped on the side read "Craftsman Electric."

"These," he asserted, "are our roof ventilation saws."

A chuckle escaped my lips before I could stop it. I waited for the punchline, for the rest of the crew to burst out laughing. But their expressions remained sincere, even proud.

My stomach churned as the reality sank in. These weren't relics or teaching tools. These nearly thirty-year-old electric saws, with their bulky extension cords, were what these men and women relied on during some of the most dangerous moments of a fire.

In that instant, a flood of emotions crashed over me – disbelief, concern, and a creeping sense of doubt about the department's leadership. But instead of probing deeper or seeking to understand, I made a critical error.

Within days of assuming my role as chief, I strode into the station with a purpose. Without explanation or discussion, I ordered the old equipment stripped from the truck. New, state-of-the-art ventilation saws soon took their place.

As I watched the crew reluctantly dismantle those obsolete reels, a nagging voice in the back of my mind whispered I'd missed an opportunity. Yes, I addressed a glaring safety issue, but at what cost? In my rush to fix what I saw as an obvious problem, I'd failed to consider the history, the reasons, or the potential wisdom behind those old saws.

Little did I know, this moment would come back to haunt me, teaching me a valuable lesson about leadership and the dangers of rushing to judgment.

Whenever an outsider takes over leadership in an organization, there's usually a damn good reason for it. Maybe a change in attitude or structure is needed, or there's no one qualified internally to step up. Whatever the reason, it's typically valid - or at least it should be. The chainsaws could've been the chance for me to illustrate the need for improvements. I could've used this as an example to the staff about the best policies and procedures, and I wanted nothing more than their safety at heart. But I didn't. I missed the boat and chose to create more problems for myself by just doing things without including anyone.

Us vs. Them

My ego and my narrow perspective saw what I wanted to see (confirmation bias), and I acted accordingly. I drove a wedge between two sides of the department: those happy to see an outsider come in to make changes, and those who felt overlooked and thought we should leave well enough alone. This rift was enhanced by my lack of communication and inability to be political, diplomatic, and empathetic.

I was taking over from a beloved chief and family member, a man who had been there for decades, knew everyone on staff, and had hired and trained most of them. I should have started by celebrating him and his achievements, memorializing his legacy, and giving him the homage he was due. This would have mended many fences and created an opportunity to share in the grieving process, supporting the staff and easing their apprehension about me.

My attitude was "Burn it all". Remember the black bunting? I put it in a box and shoved it in the basement where I thought it belongs. There's a new sheriff in town, and you all better get used to the big changes that are about to happen. Like it or not, change is a-comin! This approach might work for some organizations, but in my situation, it was totally the wrong move. I was a dead man walking. I created a wedge and a giant wall between the department and I.

The Simmer and the Boil

Leadership challenges are similar to a pot on the stove. They start as a simmer, barely noticeable if you're not paying attention. But before you know it, you've got a full boil on your hands, and you're scrambling to keep the lid on.

These challenges will occur when you're a leader, with or without your knowledge or action. Sometimes it can be a simple assumption or misinterpretation. Sometimes it's overlooking something that turns out to be important later. Whatever the reason or cause, it will happen. How you act upon it and what you do about it will determine how well it's fixed.

Challenges to your leadership don't have to be direct. They can simmer in the shadows, coming from rumors and talk among the staff. Some people love drama and will look for any chance to throw a wrench in your plans. How you address them will be closely watched. You may handle everything right and by the book, only to have them go out and tell a different story to the masses. As a leader, you've got to be ready for this treatment and develop a thick skin.

It's because of the rumor mill you can't believe everything you hear. Investigate and take time to find out the truth. What one person says will change many times after it's repeated. You'll be amazed at how often something that sounds horrible turns out to be a harmless comment that someone misinterpreted and ran with.

The best advice I can give is don't overreact. Wait, listen, and ask. If you did the right thing from the start, let your actions show it—demonstrate to your team who you are, what you stand for, and back it up with the choices you make every day. Then when something crazy is said, no one will believe it. Those looking for trouble will run with it, and you can address it with them later. But your ability to be calm under pressure will show in these situations. They're watching how you react and what you do. Be positive and be the leader you'd want to have yourself.

Integrity is Key

Life itself isn't fair; there are inequities all over. Some have good luck without much effort. Others struggle through hardship and pain just for the smallest of advances. My grandfather used to say, "if I didn't have bad luck, I'd have no luck at all." Not much in this world can be equal. But the one thing you control, as the leader, is to be fair and treat people as equally as possible in your actions. Don't treat one person better than another. Don't allow one person more leeway than another. Don't punish one action and look the other way with another. Your staff will see this inequity, the special treatment for some, and they will revolt against it. It may not be an open mutiny, but you will have an enormously hard time getting them to buy in and go along with your program. Show your good and high standards for yourself and others.

All we ever ask for is a fair shake at life. As the leader, you have the power to control that for your staff. Give them the respect they deserve. Treat them right. Find common ground. Learn and earn their trust. Once you've established that, you'll be in a far better position to achieve success by working together.

Nepotism and Favoritism

Nepotism and favoritism are also linked to the inequity thought process. In many small organizations, such as the fire department I was chief of, there can be many family members among the staff. It's especially difficult when you're asking a mother or father to be in charge of their sons or daughters. More often than not they will inherently think they deserve special treatment.

The way you can handle this type of situation is to have an honest discussion with those officers or managers. They need to understand you recognize the situation and the challenges they face, but it's essential they treat their family members the same as everyone else—no special treatment or exceptions.

Being open and honest with them will go a long way. But

empower them to make those decisions for themselves. Hold them accountable, but give them room to work and make the choices they need to. No one likes to see favoritism take place. It can destroy morale and turn a group sour on the entire organization. This will especially be true if you as the leader ignore it and do nothing about it.

Ensure everyone is treated the same and everyone has the same chances. The good ol' boy network has worked a lot in the past. I've heard the saying often "*it isn't what you know but who you know.*" That type of mentality has to go away. Leaders have to stand up and hire people and reward people for hard work and honest merit and accomplishment. Reward the ones who are most qualified and deserve the positions based on their work effort, education, and abilities. It is the right thing to do. The only way we'll ever change this world is by standing up and doing the right thing for the right reasons.

The Old Timers and the Mutiny

Sometimes, you might feel as though you're facing mutiny. I know I did. I felt the aggression, resistance, and animosity I faced were coming from a place of jealousy and resentment. The current of the river was very choppy and swift. I knew starting out I was walking into a difficult situation. The "old timers" had been in leadership positions for decades. They were all close friends and were still mourning the loss of their friend and chief.

As you've probably noticed by now, I didn't exactly get off to the best start. In fact, I practically started by sticking my size 13 right in my mouth. Looking back, I can't say for sure sitting down with them as a group or taking them out to lunch would have made a difference—but it certainly wouldn't have hurt. Ignoring them as I did was not the answer. But I felt their feelings toward me couldn't be changed. So, I chose to take the path of least resistance and just ignore them and go about my business of "fixing things". I thought maybe after seeing what I was trying to do and achieve, they might realize I had their best interests in mind. I assumed wrong.

Because I chose to identify them as the "old timers" and relegate them to being the problem, they became my scapegoat. I blamed them for all the hardships and adversity I was facing. They became an easy excuse. Without trying too hard, the younger members, who were with me in the change, started to take sides. I was creating an "us" versus "them" mentality. This led to internal strife and an atmosphere filled with tension. I created a terrible and toxic workplace.

Even though I didn't set out to do this, I achieved it with great success. It's always easier to destroy than create. If you want to create a positive and forward-facing environment, pitting one group against another will not create a successful team. I was horribly wrong in my thinking and actions. I not only facilitated the bad behavior, I also encouraged it by not addressing it and allowing it to fester and grow. I thought maybe if I made it hard for the "old timers," they would quit and leave so I could move forward faster with my changes.

But the opposite happened. They dug in, and I underestimated their political capital to influence other outside players.

The Path to Redemption

Overcoming leadership challenges starts with you. We need to be honest and open about our faults and misgivings. To be the best leader possible, we must set our own interests aside and focus on empowering and improving the group and department we've been entrusted to lead.

Stepping into a leadership role can feel like jumping into unexpected currents that catch you off guard. You assume things from shore only to find out there's an undertow or riptide when you jump in the water. If you swim against the current, you'll go nowhere and burn yourself out and drown. You've got to go with the flow for a bit, find out who those key players are, investigate the real culture, and look for yourself what challenges need to be addressed now versus later. Come up with a plan to attack the issues and then implement it, start off slowly, and take baby steps. Be patient and understand it's all a process. Sometimes those you may see as enemies at first may turn out to be great allies.

Facing an internal revolt about your decisions as a leader is hard. But ultimately, it's caused by our own actions. We've got to be accountable to what we did, how we did it, and how we communicated it, or lack thereof. Small fires spread and become bigger as time goes on. We know this all too well in the fire service. *Where there's smoke, there's fire.* Don't throw gasoline on the small fire by making arbitrary choices without input. Don't fan those flames. Think about it strategically and from a positive leadership growth mindset. You've got to step back and assess the situation. Think about the possible solutions and their effectiveness.

If your goal is to replace nearly thirty-year-old saws, then instead of just doing it yourself, start to ask about replacement and warranty work. Bring up questions such as whether the saw chain can handle the torque required to cut through multiple layers of asphalt sheeting on a roof. Talk about what happens when the extension cord gets burned. This will likely lead to someone suggesting, "Hey, we need new saws." Now it's their idea. Let them own it. Show your support by offering to help achieve the goal and set up a group to research and test new models. Let the team find the solution. This way, they have ownership and trust the team decision, not just the chief chose the saw.

I'm sure over time, the solution you had in mind will come up. But you've got to have the patience to let the process work out. It isn't worth the hassle and the revolt. Extinguish those fires before they become so consuming they take you out with them. *Work smarter, not harder.* In these instances, you've got to think about using your politician hat and go the diplomatic route. *Kill them with kindness.* But communicate your message clearly. The hardest part of communication during challenges is to listen with both ears. Don't listen to respond with your thoughts. Make a genuine effort to listen and hear what the other side is saying. If you do that with integrity and honesty, your dedication will be rewarded.

In the end, challenges to your leadership isn't about being the smartest person in the room or having all the answers. As I learned through my chaotic journey as fire chief, the best leaders aren't those who avoid making mistakes - they're the ones who learn from them and use those lessons to create stronger, more cohesive teams that can work out their own problems and issues.

Lessons Learned:

1. Addressing and resolving simmering issues early can prevent them from becoming larger problems later.

2. Integrity matters most when making decisions and being fair and open.

3. Effective communication and empathy are essential to prevent divisions and foster a united team.

Chapter 18: Politics

"IN POLITICS, NOTHING HAPPENS BY ACCIDENT. IF IT HAPPENS, YOU CAN BET IT WAS PLANNED THAT WAY."

— FRANKLIN D. ROOSEVELT

CHAPTER 18: POLITICS

October 3, 2013

It was nearly two weeks into my new position when a knock on the door disrupting my thoughts. Our village Police Chief stood in the doorway, a slight smirk on his lips. "I'm here to see the man making all the fuss," he said. "Let's take a ride." Eager for a break I jumped at the chance.

As we cruised through the village streets, the Police Chief, a veteran of several decades, shared hidden secrets and political insights. His parting wisdom was simple: "Take it slow." I heard him, but I wasn't listening. My bullheaded, demolition attitude had already made waves, and he was trying to warn me. My failure to hear his advice early on would prove to be another of my greatest mistakes.

I thought I understood the role of politics in leadership, but I had severely underestimated its significance. When you achieve a leadership position, politics becomes an inevitable part of your role, whether you like it or not. The extent of your political involvement is directly proportional to your level of responsibility. As a department Chief, I found myself embroiled in politics not just within my department, but also in village government, surrounding departments, and at the county and state levels.

Your Role in Politics

What I hate most about politics is the pandering, the lying, and the outright hypocrisy. If you despise it like me you're in for a rough ride because it will always be a major part of the leader's role. That's why it's crucial to identify the key players in the political realm: who holds power, who makes decisions, and who wields influence. Take the time to understand those parties' interests, families, hobbies, and goals. Listen carefully; you'll be amazed at how much knowledge you can gain. Politics is a game of achieving your goals through influence and strategic positioning. You won't succeed by ripping off band-aids and burning down bridges as I did.

Don't get me wrong, I'm not saying you need to become a brown-noser, but charging in with guns blazing is equally ineffective. Take the time to observe, listen, and understand the environment. Identify the potential pitfalls, the personalities, and the situations that could derail your leadership. The most effective politicians know how to navigate these treacherous waters. Set yourself up for success by being smart and patient. Time is on your side; use it wisely and understand your role in the political theatre.

CHAPTER 18: POLITICS

Working with Other Leaders

As a leader, you'll inevitably work with other department or agency heads. In my case, this included the Police Chief, the Street and Public Works Chair, and the Village President. But my sphere of influence extended far beyond these immediate contacts. I found myself interacting with neighboring fire and police departments, the county sheriff, county street and highway departments, our local Emergency Management Director, and the local power and gas agency. Add to this community groups such as health and human services, aging and disability organizations, church groups, school districts, and non-profit organizations, not to mention local businesses. The web of connections that form our society is vast and complex, and as Chief, I had to navigate and engage with nearly all of these groups at one time or another.

The sheer volume of meetings and requests to speak to me was overwhelming. Hundreds of emails flooded my inbox weekly, each demanding attention. It's impossible for one person to be an active and full participant in every request. What made my situation worse was the decision to consolidate all power and become an autocrat and dictator. I should have taken the time to understand the existing political dynamics and who was active on which committee or group. But the lack of trust I helped to create on both sides, and the festering animosity made it impossible for me to view the command staff as anything other than adversaries. I should've delegated responsibilities to them and empowered them.

Being Chief meant I needed to attend meetings, engage in discussions, and be involved in numerous issues and challenges. From coordinating with the street department about turnaround areas on a new boulevard to fulfilling requests for fire and EMS prevention talks at elder living apartments, the demands were endless. I took it upon myself to do everything, burning the candle at both ends and even starting a new wick in the middle. To be a success you need to work with others. Trust in your department leaders to take on some of the political weight. I worried they would fail and my concern became a reality when I was the one who failed. Don't fear letting others help you. Give them the chance.

Delegate in Order to be More Effective

I feared giving responsibility to others and it was a major issue for me to deal with. I knew a crucial aspect of leadership is delegating responsibilities and involving your officers and staff in the process. Even if they stumble, allowing your department leaders to take chances and learn is essential. After a few months of trying to do it all, I realized I couldn't manage alone and reluctantly relinquished control of certain aspects to individuals I knew and trusted. However, these individuals were not current officers, which led to accusations of favoritism – not entirely unfounded.

The hidden secret in politics is to make others believe an idea is their own. This is a skill I've yet to master, a true art form for which no step-by-step guide exists. It requires a certain persona to accomplish successfully. In the absence of this skill,

CHAPTER 18: POLITICS

honesty and clear communication are your best allies. With these tools, you can achieve great things as a leader. But again, patience is key.

Collaboration with other departments and agencies is essential. I discovered we're all in the same boat, each feeling alone and in need of support. This realization hit home during my meetings with a fire chief from a neighboring town. We would brainstorm ideas and engage in communal reflection, a valuable exercise in problem-solving. He took a slower, more measured approach compared to my breakneck pace of ripping off band-aids. Unsurprisingly, his method proved more effective, and he remains a respected fire chief to this day. He understood the power political delegation can bring and used it to his advantage.

It's remarkable how universal thoughts and fears are among agency and department leaders. Remember, you're not alone in this process, and it's okay to ask for help. My mistake was thinking I had to do everything independently. My worrisome attitude and lack of faith in my command staff made things harder than they needed to be. Work with the team you have and find common ground. Communicate honestly and openly. Delegate the tasks you don't have time for but also be mindful not to dump all the "crappy tasks" on your staff. Be cognizant of what you are delegating and why.

Use Diplomacy in Politics

Diplomacy isn't owned solely by the politicians. Being diplomatic means you can set aside ego and emotional connection to events or issues, to rationally think and understand the underlying consequences and actions. But even more, it is tied to communication. I failed to see this and realize my larger role and potential. I failed to be empathetic. I failed to be rational. As the leader, I should've brought all interested parties, the stakeholders, into a meeting to talk about what the problems and challenges were, to find a common interest and to find a resolution. Even if it had no chance to work, I should have been the better person and at the very least tried.

Politics is a massive component of leadership, one I failed to navigate successfully. My inability to see past my own ego and righteousness caused damage and detracted from the good I was genuinely trying to accomplish. I chose a direct path, believing it to be more efficient, but it proved to be far more difficult and destructive than necessary.

In retrospect, the challenges I faced were largely of my own making. My choices and lack of political awareness cost me dearly. The lesson here is clear: effective leadership requires not just vision and determination, but also political expertise, patience, and the ability to communicate diplomatically with groups. It's about building bridges, not burning them down; about bringing people along with you, not charging ahead alone.

As leaders, we must remember that change, no matter how

necessary, is often met with resistance. Our job is not just to identify what needs to be done, but to bring others on board. This requires tact, empathy, and often, a willingness to compromise or at least to proceed at a pace that allows others to adapt which is the essence of a good diplomatic mission.

The political aspect of leadership should not be about manipulation or deceit. At its best, it's about understanding the needs, fears, and motivations of others, and finding ways to align these with the goals of the organization. It's about building consensus, fostering trust, and creating an environment where change is seen as an opportunity rather than a threat.

My experience as a Fire Chief taught me political diplomacy is as much about people as it is about policies or procedures. The technical knowledge of fire safety codes and best practices was important, but equally crucial was the ability to navigate the human elements of the job – the relationships, the power dynamics, and the emotional responses to your communication and messaging.

Collaboration is Key in Partnerships

This leads us directly to the importance of collaboration and building alliances. My ego and failure to bring my command staff on board hindered my achievements. Collaboration, like communicating an engaging message, is key. Politics revolves around working with people who may think differently or have conflicting agendas. The ability to set aside animosity and focus on shared beliefs is crucial. We all want to make a difference, help as many people as possible, and do our best. Our commonalities often outweigh our disagreements. The challenge lies in looking past contentious issues and working together to achieve success toward a common goal.

Working with others demands patience. As a leader, you must see beyond your interests, remain calm, practice humility, and step back when necessary. Winning isn't everything. Sometimes, it's about minimizing losses. Think of those nail-biting sports moments where the final play determines the outcome. We sit on the edge of our seats, hoping for victory, only to experience either cheerful joy or crushing defeat. Collaboration isn't this black and white. Politics operates in shades of gray. We may achieve some of our goals, but not all.

Partnerships can make or break your success. A capable leader assembles a diverse group of people to achieve their goals. Remember, you don't have to do it all alone. Invite others to help, especially those with knowledge you may lack. Check your ego and let go of the need for absolute control. Partners can support you in numerous ways. I wish I had realized this earlier in my career. I often wonder how much more successful I could have been if I had embraced partnerships to facilitate necessary changes. My command staff, with their individual strengths, could have made my job significantly easier. Instead of fighting them, I should have won them over with kindness and invited them to join me in elevating the department to its full potential.

Seeking partners isn't a sign of weakness; it strengthens your position. Communicate your desires and ask around. A simple question can take you far. Collaborate and find ways to work with as many different people as possible. Create new alliances and establish strong foundations for future projects. Politics will always play a role in leadership positions. Whether it helps or hurts you is in your control.

Being an Effective Political Leader

Most importantly, never lose sight of the fact leadership is ultimately about service – to your team, your organization, and your community. When politics becomes about personal gain rather than collective benefit, we lose our way as leaders.

As I reflect on my time as Fire Chief, I realize my greatest regret is not the mistakes I made, but the opportunities I missed – opportunities to build stronger relationships, create a positive environment, and effect change in a way that brought people together rather than dividing them and driving them apart.

Embrace the political aspects of leadership, but with integrity, empathy, and a genuine desire to serve. In doing so, you'll not only be more effective as a leader, but you'll also find greater fulfillment in your role, knowing you're making a positive difference in the lives of those you lead and serve.

Lessons Learned:

1. Never underestimate your political influence on others and the situation you are in. Communication and patience are keys to success.

2. Working with other government leaders and department heads can be challenging if you don't understand their purpose, politics, and positions.

3. Collaborate and find partners to help you. Scratch backs and help as much as you can but also don't be afraid to ask for help in return.

Chapter 19: Failure

"FAILURE SHOULD BE OUR TEACHER, NOT OUR UNDERTAKER. FAILURE IS DELAY, NOT DEFEAT. IT IS A TEMPORARY DETOUR, NOT A DEAD END."

— DENIS WAITLEY

CHAPTER 19: FAILURE

September 11, 2014

The board room was as quiet as a tomb. There were three members present, the village president, the PFC chairman, and another PFC member. They sat in a row at the meeting table, their faces unreadable, while I sat opposite them, strangely my palms weren't sweating and my heart wasn't beating out of my chest.

I already knew the outcome.

The PFC's report was sitting neatly in front of the president, but I didn't need to read it to know what it said. I had made too many mistakes, created too much animosity, and burned too many bridges. They had decided to eliminate my full-time chief position. They chose to return to a part-time chief role, and they were asking for my resignation. A formality, really. A polite way of saying it was time for me to go.

As the words fell from the president's mouth, I sat there, silent, nodding along as if I were listening. But in reality, my thoughts were elsewhere—thinking about every decision

I had made in the last year. The late nights, the tough calls, the moments I thought I had it all figured out. The weight of responsibility I had carried for so long suddenly felt like it had been lifted off my shoulders. But the relief left behind a dull ache, a hole of failure in my spirit.

"Thank you for all you've done," the PFC chairman concluded. And that was it.

I stood, shook hands, and walked out of the room. Outside, I closed my eyes and faced the late afternoon sun. I took a deep breath and walked to my car.

In the days and weeks that followed, I watched as they made their decisions—ultimately choosing to combine with the neighboring department, creating a new fire district.

For weeks, the questions circled in my mind—what had gone wrong? Every failure seemed to replay in vivid detail, every misstep magnified in hindsight. I had been focused on pushing forward, on achieving my vision, I hadn't seen the cracks forming underneath me, ready to swallow me up.

But here's the thing about failure—it teaches you more than success ever could. Not immediately though. At first, it just sucks. But over time, you begin to see the lessons through the pain. I didn't need anyone to tell me where I went wrong. The answers were there, buried in every decision I had made, every meeting I had walked into without listening, every conversation I had rushed through in the name of efficiency.

That's why I'm writing this book. Not to tell you what to do, but to show you what **NOT** to do. To remind you failure isn't an endpoint, but a stepping stone. We all fall. It's part of the process. What matters is how you pick yourself up and learn why you fell.

Reach for the Stars

Take the mirror test daily, and evaluate yourself. Assess the actions you've taken and look for ways to improve. There's always something to get better at. Learning and education are lifelong processes. We'll never know everything. New information is discovered daily, expanding knowledge in every field. Become a subject matter expert. Learn and continue to learn. Reevaluate what you know and build on your understanding. Growth is a mindset every great leader needs to adopt.

I know this now in hindsight, but I wish I'd been smart enough to realize it at the time. When you think positively, good things usually happen. When you think negatively, negative things will occur. Call it a self-fulfilling prophecy, but we attract whatever we choose to concentrate on. Why not choose something positive? I'm not saying you'll have all positive days, but I am saying to look at bad situations and find the positive in them. How you look at the world is up to you.

A great team with a positive environment relishes learning and the ability to improve. They don't shy away from failure but embrace it. They use it to challenge themselves to be greater. They see failure as a stepping stone on their way to victory. How would you want a leader to respond to failure? Ignore it and just keep doing what you've been doing? They often say in the fire service there are only two things firefighters hate: the way things are and change.

Embrace your Mistakes

It's easy to complain about mistakes, to second-guess, and Monday morning quarterback situations. To talk a big game and say how you would've done something different. But when you're in the real position to make those calls, when the pressure is on, how will you react? Are you prepared? Do you have enough gumption and fortitude to act? Failure teaches and is the best motivator for improvement. Sometimes we have to fail in order to grow. Accept it and embrace it.

In General Schwarzkopf's book, *It Doesn't Take a Hero*, he wrote we all learn far more from negative leadership and failure. He stated, "Because you learn how not to do it. And, therefore learn how to do it." We have to be comfortable with screwing things up and making mistakes. Not only with our own choices but with allowing failure in others. Our staff needs to know they will make mistakes and they need to learn from them. They can't fear this failure. If they do, they won't act or make decisions because they fear being scolded or criticized. Failure must be embraced as the learning opportunity it is. As young students, we all make mistakes in school. The role of the teacher isn't to come down hard on them and slap their hands, but to support them in their growth. We want smart and capable staff to perform their work successfully, achieve goals, and contribute to the positive well-being of the department. If you create a negative atmosphere where failure is seen as a detriment, then you're missing an opportunity for growth.

Learning to step back and allow mistakes to happen takes patience and foresight. You may even give a task to someone you know will fail. That's okay. The hope is through failure, growth will happen and learning will occur, allowing the person to be better for it. It's hard to do. Don't see their failure as a failure on your part. Sure, there are instances where you obviously wouldn't allow someone unqualified or unfit to make a major mistake. But with other tasks and mundane work, there's plenty of opportunity for learning and growth.

Learning to Grow

It was late in the third quarter, and the NFL's Cincinnati Bengals were locked in a fierce battle with the Oakland Raiders in the early 1970s. The football game was incredibly close. Coach Bill Walsh, the Bengals Offensive Coordinator, called a standard pass play. Tight End Bob Trumpy was supposed to line up on the right side of the formation. However, amid the deafening crowd noise and intensity of the game in Oakland, Trumpy misheard the play call and lined up on the wrong side.

Realizing his mistake at the last moment, Trumpy scrambled to the correct side of the formation just before the snap. This sudden movement threw the Raiders' defense into confusion. The Raiders relied heavily on specialized defensive roles: a weak-side linebacker, a strong-side linebacker, and a defensive end who played on the tight-end side.

As Trumpy sprinted across the formation, the Raiders' defenders scrambled to adjust. Linebackers and defensive backs collided with each other in a frantic attempt to realign themselves. The chaos created a moment of opportunity. Bengals Quarterback Virgil Carter, seizing the chance, snapped the ball and quickly fired a pass, taking advantage of the disorganized defense and gaining significant yardage for a first down.

What had been an accident revealed a powerful discovery, intentional motion of the offense could confuse defenses, force them to reveal their schemes, and create mismatches. By incorporating tight end motion into their playbook, the Bengals could exploit these opportunities and gain a tactical edge.

This accidental innovation underscored a fundamental truth: failure, when embraced and examined, can lead to groundbreaking success. The confusion caused by Trumpy's unplanned motion revealed how rigid and specialized defenses could be exploited. This type of activity had never been done in the NFL or football before. Walsh's willingness to learn from this mistake and transform it into a strategic advantage exemplifies the importance of embracing and learning from failure.

CHAPTER 19: FAILURE

This belief ties in with how you view failure as a leader. The power to embrace failure should be part of your organization. Illustrate and communicate how everyone needs to reflect and review decisions. Learn from them and advance ourselves and our departments. Organizing such a program can create opportunities for experienced members to grow as teachers and leaders. Empower your members to look for opportunities to challenge themselves. Allow them to seek out new knowledge, and attend workshops, or conferences. Have them report back regularly on what they found. Creating an environment where learning from failure and mistakes is encouraged will strengthen your leadership style and reinforce your organizational strategy.

As leaders, we can do a lot to create this positive growth mindset. As chief, I didn't even think about it. I took for granted the experience I had sitting in front of me. I failed to see the value in my veterans. I didn't review my own actions. I didn't inspire creation, didn't allow flexibility, didn't promote professional growth, and didn't collaborate. Those are all things I should have done from day one. As chief, it was my job to do so. That being said, it all didn't have to happen all at once. Give yourself time to make the necessary changes to achieve those goals. Find out how others can help you, and how they can support you. And tell them how you'll need their support and help in return.

Creating this attitude will take time. Small steps lead to big gains. You will stumble and you will fall. Pick yourself up and learn from your mistakes. Grow yourself and show your staff it's okay to fail. Foster the growth mindset and embrace change and improvement. We can either roll with the changes and adapt to our surroundings, or we can go extinct. The choice is up to you.

Lessons Learned:

1. Continually learn and become better at what limits you.

2. Accept and embrace your mistakes and failures, they can become your greatest teacher.

3. Create a positive learning environment for everyone to try new ideas and to attempt new responsibilities.

Chapter 20: Balance

> "WHEN YOU SAY 'YES' TO OTHERS, MAKE SURE YOU ARE NOT SAYING 'NO' TO YOURSELF."
>
> — PAULO COELHO

CHAPTER 20: BALANCE

After taking over as President of the United States following the assassination of William McKinley in 1901, Theodore Roosevelt encountered repeated personal tragedies. In a single day, both his wife and mother died, two of the most important people in his life. The weight of those losses hit him hard forcing him to confront just how fragile life is.

But Roosevelt wasn't one to wear his emotions on his sleeve. As a "Rough Rider," he embodied the American ideal of strength, toughness, and action. His political marketing campaign pushed this "tough guy" image, so he had to put on a brave face, holding it all together as the world watched, but deep down, the grief deeply hit him. And while he was known for charging forward, this pain made him pause and reflect on his own balances. He began to realize no matter how demanding his position, no matter how significant his role as President, he couldn't ignore the need to care for himself and those he loved. He had to find a true balance.

For Roosevelt, balance came through what he famously called "The Strenuous Life." He believed in working hard, but he also believed in living a full life. Hunting, boxing, hiking, and writing weren't just hobbies, they were part of his balance with work. On every trip to the outdoors he would bring his family along. They kept him grounded, gave him perspective, and made him a better leader and father. And because he found peace in the natural world, he became a fierce advocate for conservation, establishing the National Park System many of us enjoy today.

The lesson here isn't just about Roosevelt's love of the outdoors; it's about making time for the things that feed your own soul. Roosevelt understood the only way to be the person, and leader, he needed to be was to prioritize his own well-being. It wasn't selfish. It was about survival.

So, ask yourself this important question: How much time are you making for your own well-being? Not the time that checks a box. I'm talking about real, honest time that recharges you. Are you making choices that make you feel alive, and remind you of who you are outside of your work? Because if Roosevelt could find time while running the country, then we have no excuse.

The Impact of Imbalance on Relationships

I've been down the road where work consumes everything. I poured all my energy into my position, convinced it was the way to succeed, the way to prove my worth. But what I didn't see then was how much I was sacrificing along the way. My relationships suffered. I became irritable, distant, and to be honest it was a version of myself I barely recognized.

CHAPTER 20: BALANCE

And the people I loved most? They bore the brunt of it. My short temper overshadowed moments that should've been filled with joy and connection. I was physically present but emotionally absent, and it hurt them more than I realized at the time.

I came home after a particularly bad day, and one of my daughters ran up to me, excited to show me something she'd made in school. But I was exhausted. I barely looked at her, brushed her off with a "I'll look at it later," and went to bury myself in more work on my computer. I didn't notice the way her shoulders slumped or how she quietly walked away. It hit me later, in the quiet of my bed, how many of those moments I'd been missing, how many I'd lost because I thought my work was more important than being present with the people I love. I was making the wrong choices and sacrificing time I could never and will never get back.

Roosevelt's experience illustrates a universal truth: no amount of professional success can make up for the loss of meaningful personal connection. He faced tragedy, but he didn't let it consume him. Instead, he leaned into what mattered, his passions, his family relationships, his sense of purpose. He didn't see nurturing those connections as distractions from his role as President; he saw them as essential to sustaining it. And that's something I had to learn the hard way.

Strategies for Achieving Balance

When I finally realized my focus on work was hurting more than helping, I knew I had to make a changes. It wasn't easy, and it didn't happen overnight, but I started to reclaim some sense of balance. Here are some of the practical steps that helped me along the way:

1. Setting Boundaries:
I realized without clear boundaries, work would always bleed into every aspect of my life. I started small. I made a rule: no checking emails after 6 PM. At first, it felt impossible. My mind was still buzzing with work, and I felt I was letting things slip through the cracks. But then something happened, I started noticing my kids more, really noticing them. And those few hours each evening? They became the most important part of my day.

2. Delegation and Trust:
For the longest time, I thought I had to do everything myself. If it wasn't done by me, it wasn't done right, or so I believed. But that mindset added to my stress and isolation. I had to learn to delegate, to trust others with responsibilities. It wasn't just about lightening my workload; it was about building a sense of trust and collaboration within my team. And the shift? It made me a better leader and gave me the breathing room I desperately needed.

3. Self-Care Rituals:
Incorporating self-care into my daily routine became non-negotiable. Whether it was taking a walk, lifting

weights, reading a book, or picking up an old hobby, these moments of "me time" allowed me to recharge and approach challenges with renewed energy and a clear mind. I had to learn self-care wasn't a luxury; it was a necessity.

These steps weren't just about finding balance, they were about preserving my sanity and strengthening my relationships. You simply must find time for yourself. It doesn't count if it's at work or while you're working. The time needs to be honest and true. And it needs to be done no matter what. Involve your family and friends. Ask them to keep you honest with it and to be present in the moments you have with them.

Long-Term Consequences of Imbalance

If you don't find balance you will inevitably become burned out. The repercussions of burnout extend far beyond those immediate stresses. Clinical research shows chronic stress can lead to physical health issues and makes you susceptible to cardiac disease and other chronic illnesses. Mentally, it diminishes our cognitive abilities, impairing decision-making and creativity—the qualities essential for effective leadership.

By nurturing our physical, emotional, and spiritual health, we fortify ourselves against the pressures of leadership and enhance our capability to inspire and lead others. Theodore Roosevelt's example and my personal journey underscore the vital importance of achieving and maintaining work-life balance. As leaders, we have a responsibility to our professional roles but also to ourselves and our loved ones. We are more than our titles and positions; we are the guardians of our own well-being and the well-being of those around us. Share this message with your team members. Show them they too need balance and tell them what you are doing to keep it. Inspire action and be the example to follow.

Finding balance isn't a one-time achievement, it's an ongoing commitment to honoring our priorities and nurturing our whole-body health. By embracing this principle we increase our effectiveness as leaders but also enrich our lives with meaning and fulfillment.

Bringing it Full Circle

In the words of President Roosevelt, "Far and away the best prize that life offers is the chance to work hard at work worth doing." But what he didn't mention is working hard doesn't mean sacrificing everything else. The real reward lies in finding the balance between hard work and living life to its fullest—between professional ambition and personal joy. This balance is what truly sustains us as leaders and as individuals.

The goal of this book is to inspire you to achieve more and become the best version of yourself. It's about being confident in your role, making bold decisions, learning from my mistakes, and guiding your organization forward. Equally important is the wisdom to understand how humility can enhance your leadership. Humility grounds you, allowing you to stay open to learning and growth.

I want you to learn from my experiences and what I've

learned through all of my setbacks. Just remember, you don't have to reinvent the wheel. Learn from the leaders who have paved the road before us. Absorb their lessons and apply them, but always recognize learning is ongoing. There is always more to discover, more to achieve, and more to understand.

Lessons Learned:

1. Create time for yourself and your family to be together. Set clear boundaries for work and home life and stick to the plan.

2. Accept failures and focus energy on growth and learning. Share what you learn and lead by example.

3. Find a balance between your work and stress-relieving hobbies and activities to ensure you have a healthy body and mind.

Epilogue

January 20, 2024

It's been ten years since I was Fire Chief and I regret a lot about what happened in my time as a leader. I did a lot, and I learned a lot in that small closet office. I made a ton of mistakes and failed at almost every turn. However, I used these instances to grow myself and to become a better leader. I wouldn't be where I am today if the chief experience hadn't happened. I wouldn't have written this book that's for sure!

I look upon that time as a tribulation which created the person I am today. I became more patient, more reserved, less bullheaded, and I learned a great deal about effective communication and to stop listening to your ego. But what I learned most is being a leader is all about the people you serve. It's your staff and your crew you lead, and it is their interests that are the most important.

With all of my training, education, and experience I thought I was ready for the job. Far from it. The fact I was trained and knew better makes it worse. But I hope as you've read about all of these issues and challenges I faced and created, you have learned from them. Leadership is a tough position. Some people have natural talents for it and some of us have to work hard every day. Use these lessons to help yourself be better and to inspire your staff to be the best they can be.

Where should you go next?

Have a conversation with yourself.

Write down the key points and keep the list with you. Or you could text yourself or email yourself. I know I do when I get inspiration, an idea, or something hits me. I send myself an email and then just reply to it over and over. That way you have what struck you. Otherwise, you'll forget it and regret it later.

Go back and ask yourself what you want in life and what you want to achieve in this leadership role you are in. How you get there can take many forms. Ask around and find out what other people have done. Contact me, I'd be more than happy to be a sounding board as you find the answers you seek.

The main thing is to never settle and to always look to improve yourself. Life is far too short to go through it without experiencing the joys it can bring. Have fun and make sure you are doing things you enjoy. If not at least try to make them fun. There's a lot to say about making a bad day into a good one. As they say, *it's better to have a rainy day on vacation than a sunny day at work.* It's all about how you look at the situation. Your attitude and your outlook is totally in your control.

Until next time. Stay safe!

Marc

APPENDIX

The following is my resignation letter to the board. Even now, as I read it, it's painfully clear I hadn't yet learned the lessons I needed to. I was still blind to the mess I had created and the trouble my leadership caused. It's honestly shocking to look back and see how stubborn and short-sighted I was. I shake my head, wondering how I missed it all—so much potential, yet I was too proud to recognize the real opportunities right in front of me.

September 12, 2014

President and PFC Chair:

Please accept this letter as my official resignation from the position of Fire Chief of the Rothschild Fire Department. As per the request to resign has come from the Police and Fire Commission meeting on September 11, 2014. I want to thank you for your support and decision to bring me on as your

Chief even though I came from outside the department. I also want to thank you both for resisting the private efforts to undermine my authority and compromise my leadership of this department as we endeavored to move in a progressive and modernized fashion. Even though the decision to bring me in as Chief was one that never had the full support of current command staff members I think it would be fair to say that those members had a vocal and aggressive minority to which fought many of the needed changes for this department. The changes I have made were necessary and the changes that still need to be made are ones that will need your continued support. The safety and the future of the department rest with continuing the progressive nature of the adjustments.

Effective immediately my personal effort to improve and progress the Rothschild Fire Department is over. I believe I did the best job I could with the circumstances that were given to me. I enjoyed my time with the department members and with the Village staff.

I wish you the best of luck.

Sincerely,

Marc Hill, M.Ed., Paramedic

Chief of Fire & EMS

Rothschild Fire Department

Please Leave a Review

If you enjoyed reading this book, please leave a review on Amazon or Goodreads. I read every review and they help new readers discover my books, positive or negative comments are pleasantly accepted. Links are below:

Amazon Reviews

https://www.amazon.com

Goodreads Reviews

https://www.goodreads.com

About Marc Hill

Marc Hill has spent over twenty years in public service. He has taught every grade from middle through high school and college-level students. In both small rural and larger urban settings. Marc has also served as an assistant coach, head coach, union president, principal, training officer, engineer, preceptor, and mentor. He has been selected as teacher of the year three times by his students. Marc also served as a volunteer firefighter and EMT before becoming a full-time Fire Chief and now retired from the City of Wausau as a firefighter and paramedic where he earned the department's merit of core values award. He is the chief instructor and founder of Two Dark Thirty: Leadership & Learning Solutions and is an adjunct instructor for General Studies & Fire/EMS at Northcentral Technical College.

Marc's passion for learning and serving inspired him to become an author writing his first book, Two Dark Thirty, and its accompanying workbook as well as the All-In-One Firefighter Preparation Book. Marc lives in Rib Mountain Wisconsin and is happily married and has three beautiful daughters.